Basic Function:
A Value Analysis Novel

James M. Guyette, Jr.

DEDICATION

To Julieta

ACKNOWLEDGMENTS

I think writing a book is the closet a man can get to experiencing natural childbirth. I would like to acknowledge my family who coached me through the birthing process.

This novel allows you to understand how Value Engineers think and solve complex problems. As you progress in your reading you soon learn to appreciate many of the key elements of Value Analysis. It includes the Why-How Logic which is the primary technique to expand your creativity into new areas of your project, not normally explored when analyzing a project or procedure. It also asks many other thought provoking questions that forces you to think more deeply about your project, like thinking in functions.

The first and most important element in analyzing a project is to be able to express you project using a new method of thinking. This new method of thinking expands your creative opportunities far beyond what people normally do. You as well as the main character in this novel learn of this new method of thinking during a Value Analysis workshop. The process of thinking in functions is very simple and only uses active verbs and nouns that can be acted upon. This dynamic method of thinking can change your life. At least it changed my life.

I'm sure you will appreciate the author's ability to humanize this novel in a typical working environment filled with hopes, fears and office politics.

Charles W. Bytheway
Inventor of FAST Diagramming

O you possessed of sturdy intellect,
Observe the teaching that is hidden here…
Beneath the veil of verses so obscure - Dante

1

I squeezed into my coffee-stained seat hoping I would have the whole row to myself. I was anxious to fly in more ways than one. I was fresh out of Embry-Riddle University, with a Bachelor of Science degree in mechanical engineering. Here I was, twenty-two, and hired for an engineering job in Chicago, my hometown, with an aerospace design firm, Alarum Aerospace, Inc. I couldn't wait to finally take my place in a world I loved.

"Excuse me."

"Yes?"

"I hate to ask, but would you mind if I sat near the window? I think I might feel less worried about flying. My name is Sally."

Sally looked to be about sixty-five or so. She was dressed in a casual pantsuit. Her greasy grey hair was smoothed back and caught in a bun near the nape of her neck. She was pale with grey eyes and seemed a little shaky as she breathed short, quick breaths.

"Hi, I'm Michelle. Of course I don't mind. Are you all right?"

"I'm nervous on an airplane, that's all. Are you going to Chicago for business or pleasure?"

"Both. Don't worry. You'll be fine. It's much safer to fly than it is to drive. I'll help you on the flight if you need me," I said as we exchanged seats.

I hope she didn't get sick or, worse, I hope she doesn't want to chat. My mind was on my new job, and I wanted to think about what it would be like to work with serious professionals, to solve problems, to be able to create. I'm a woman, in a field dominated by men, and I'm not exactly a pushy type. I'm not a pushover, either, though. Will they accept me? The butterflies in my stomach took flight the moment I said yes to this opportunity. Dammit! I know my stuff. They'll see.

My thoughts were interrupted by the captain's amplified voice over the speakers. "Good morning, ladies and gentlemen." *It always sounds like the pilots are screaming or whispering never anything in between.* "Welcome to UN, Flight 465 to Chicago. Make sure your seats are upright and your belts are buckled. Sit back, relax and enjoy your flight."

The seat belt sign went on, and the flight attendants sat down after completing their safety briefing. We taxied to the runway leaving the hot and sticky Florida weather behind. Sally took a deep breath and braced herself. Both hands gripped the armrests, and she stared straight ahead. For the first time, I saw what "white knuckle flier" meant. The engines revved up, and we started to move, then came to a stop in a short distance.

Sally turned to me. "What's the matter? Why did they stop? Is something wrong?"

"Oh, no. We're fine," I assured her. "We must be in a line with other planes. The tower will tell the pilot when it's our turn to leave safely."

She didn't answer. She went back to staring at nothing and tightened her hands on the armrests. *I wonder what she's thinking?*

Our plane waited, positioned for permission to take off, like a bird anxious to join its flock. Then we rolled again. This time, we made the turn onto the runway and, after a split second's hesitation, began to gather speed, until . . . lift-off! The plane's nose pointed toward heaven. The whine of the wheels pulling up startled Sally. She gasped, taking her first breath since taxing to the runway.

"What was that? Did we hit something?"

"It's okay, Sally." I smiled, hoping to relax her. "It was the wheels. They were tucked away. We won't need them for a while."

I glanced up in time to see the seat belt sign turn off. I heard a chorus of clicks as passengers made themselves comfortable, pulled out newspapers, magazines, books, or just settled back for a nap. I closed my eyes and started to relax, too. Soon we were sailing smoothly at 37,000 feet.

Then . . . My God! The bottom dropped out. It was more like a plunge. I felt like I was riding the world's tallest rollercoaster. We must have dropped hundreds of feet in less than a second. Oxygen masks fell from the ceiling like prizes from a piñata. I reached for one and put it on. I grabbed the seat in front of me as I was thrown forward, glad that I was still belted in. I took a quick look at Sally. Her belt was on, too. It held her. Her eyes were closed and her arms flailed in synch with the gyrations of our plane. Perhaps she fainted during the fall. I struggled to get hold of her mask to fit it on her face.

The sights and sounds were that of a war movie. People screamed as if they were being tortured. Some held their ears; some threw up. The stench was terrible. Mothers grabbed their crying babies and held on as tight as they could. A nun in a forward seat prayed the rosary. I watched in horror as some unbelted passengers flew into the air and hit the ceiling and the open doors of the overhead luggage compartments; others without seat belts were flung around the cabin like rag dolls; loose items became projectiles and scattered everywhere, as if it were the Mayan prediction of the end of the world by gravity reversal. The interior began to break up all over. I had the feeling it wouldn't be long before the rest of it went, too. I was paralyzed with the images in front of my eyes. I looked at my hands that gripped the seat. My knuckles were as white as Sally's, and I began to tremble. I feared how this would end.

Then as quickly as it began, it ended. The pilots somehow stabilized the plane, held it, and the plane leveled off flying smoothly again. We came down thousands of feet in an instant, where we were able to breathe normally. We were told we were going to make an emergency landing. Sally and I were still belted in our seats, shaken but unhurt. *Mental note: listen to the safety briefing before next flight…if there's a next flight.*

As we rolled toward the end of the runway, I could see all the ambulances and fire trucks waiting. I caught a name on the side of a truck, Orlando Fire Department. We hadn't even left Florida! As soon as we came to a full stop, a world of care descended on us. Mercifully, Sally was out through the whole thing. I hoped it wasn't her heart, though, and that at worst she just fainted from the shock. In any event, I was sure she would never fly again. I saw one of the many ambulance drivers begin to take her away on a gurney. I ran to grab him.

"Excuse me, can you tell me where you are taking her? She is a friend of mine."

"That will be the Orlando hospital. Near here, Ma'am."

"Thank you," I called as they sped away. I made a mental note to phone and check on her later. I was told about forty people were taken to other area hospitals and treated. Some had serious injuries. Authorities insisted I get checked, as well. I felt okay and refused treatment.

It dawned on me, after I caught my breath, my parents must have heard about this disaster since they were planning to pick me up at O'Hare. I pulled out my phone and dialed.

"Mom? It's Michelle . . . I know . . . I know, Mom. It's okay. Don't cry. I'm fine . . . Yes, I was checked. I'm fine . . . Where am I? Orlando, Florida. That's where we emergency landed, but there will be a plane to Chicago for those of us who can leave. Can Dad still pick me up at O'Hare? . . . Tell him I'll call when I get there. . I love you, too, Mom."

When I reached Chicago and claimed my luggage, the second call I made was the Orlando Hospital. How naïve was I to think they would give me the status of a passenger whose first name was all I knew? I was relieved to hear that everyone was in stable condition and only a few passengers would have to stay the night. I'm sure Sally is fine and I'm sure she will be taking the train the rest of the way to Chicago.

I had a jumble of thoughts while I waited for my Dad, and again after our hugs and kisses, and we were on our way home. *What will my new boss be like? What will my first project be? Do I ever want to fly again? I wonder what's for dinner? How long until I can afford my own place to live? Will I ever be able to wipe the horrible images from the rapid decompression from my mind's eye?*

"You're unusually quiet. Do you want to talk about it?"

"Not yet. You know, Dad, I missed you guys. I know it's only been a few days since graduation. But I really missed you."

"Oh, Princess, we missed you, too. Welcome home."

"Thanks…and thanks to you and mom for driving my car back home." *I didn't even have enough gas money to drive my car home. How long until I get my first paycheck?*

It had only been a few months since I was last back home, but when we merged onto the expressway, things somehow didn't look the same. It's funny how the night can disorient you, and its bright lights along the way can send your thoughts in a whole different direction than they would in daylight. It's even funnier how Chicago traffic can be worse at night than it is during the day – just two seasons in Chicago: winter and road construction season.

This was an auspicious beginning to my new life in Chicago. I crossed my fingers and prayed it wasn't a sign of things to come. But what caused this disaster? I needed to know. I'm an engineer. That's why I'm here. What if I can be the one to keep things like this from ever happening again, or at least be part of that team? What if it were some small part that went rogue and set off a chain reaction that no one could imagine? What if . . . *I'll go straight to bed when I get home. I have to be on the job early.*

2

"Good morning," I said to the receptionist. It was 8:59 A.M., and I was just in time, in spite of last night's horror . . . or maybe because of it. I felt as if I had a mission. "I'm here to see Mr. Davis."

"You must be Ms. Jamison?"

"Yes, I'm Michelle Jamison."

"Of course, Ms. Jamison. He's expecting you. Have a seat, won't you? He'll be right out." Her voice was as pleasant as her smile, in an efficient sort of way. Her movements as she spoke displayed the self-confidence of someone who knew what her position demanded.

A tall, slim, grey-haired man of about sixty, wearing a trim, dark suit that complemented his frame, strode out of his office. He had a heavy step for a man of his build. It sounded like he was marching with concrete shoes. You felt his footsteps as much as you heard them. With a smile on his face, he extended his hand to shake mine. If I were at all nervous, his whole manner put me at ease.

"I'm Dean Davis. Glad that you've joined us, Ms. Jamison," his voice boomed, "and it couldn't be at a better time." The volume of his voice matched the weight of his step.

I smiled. "Michelle, please."

"All right. I'd give you the grand tour, Michelle, but we're about to leave for a nearby community college for a little workshop we've set up. We decided to hold it there, because we thought people might be more creative away from their normal work environment and its distractions. You'll meet some of our staff there, and I'll show you around later. In the meantime, let me take you to your office, and you can settle in. I believe we're due at the workshop about 10:00. Am I right Sue?" He didn't have to raise his voice to get her attention.

"Yes, sir!" She had to raise hers.

"I'll come and collect you when it's time. Sue is my right hand, Michelle. Great gal. You'll be seeing a lot of her around here."

"Nice to meet you, Sue."

Mr. Davis ushered me out, and we started for whatever cubicle would be mine, when we were stopped by a frazzled looking man, built like a small tank. His shirt collar was pulled open, his tie was loose, and his frown threatened to find a permanent home on his forehead.

"Hey, Bob! You going to the workshop?"

"Yeah. Do I have a choice? I tell you, I'm not happy about it. This is such a waste of time. I have designs to release, non-conformance rejection documents to disposition and airplanes to build. Instead I have to sit there and listen to some consultant tell me how to build airplanes."

"You never know. You might learn something."

"Yeah, yeah, yeah" he said, throwing up his hands.

"Michelle, meet our one and only Bob Green, giving you a bad impression. And this, Mr. Green, is Michelle Jamison. She's a mechanical engineer who started with us today."

"That's nice. Good luck." He walked away with a scowl, still mumbling under his breath.

Mr. Davis chuckled as we continued on our way. "That's Bob," he said. "He's the chief engineer for Environmental Control Systems. He's been here only thirty years. By the way you're to work with him in his department. Don't worry though. His heart's in the right place. It's his head I worry about sometimes."

"Oh!"

True to his word, Mr. Davis came by at the appointed time for the workshop meeting at the community college. He had explained to me that a consultant was there to introduce and demonstrate a concept that might improve our potential. He called it Value Analysis. I was excited, because I had heard of it in school, and I was eager to learn its practical application.

The familiar smell of books and paper greeted us when we walked in. It almost made me feel homesick for the school where my life had been centered for the last four years. The unfamiliar smell was machine oil from the static teardown of several Alarum components. It made me feel excited for beginning my career in aerospace engineering. The other staff were already there, and all eyes turned to me. But was I intimidated? You bet! I lifted my chin, walked clear across the room and took a seat in one of the chairs arranged around a large, oblong, conference-room-type table. I scanned the group. No one looked happy to be there, least of all with someone new in their midst, and a female, at that.

The seven-team members were all talking. They didn't realize how audible they were, even when they whispered, and that included Bob. Still grumpy, he looked one of the men up and down and said, "How come you're not wearing a tie?"

"This is a casual dress company, remember, Bob? How come you're wearing one?"

"It makes me feel more professional, okay?" He eyed the consultant and said, "Geez, he doesn't have one on, either."

The group groused a lot:

"Look at him! Is he kidding? I have underwear older than he is."

"What are we, back in school again? I've been here seventeen years."

"Let's ask him to sit down. I can teach the course."

Here and there, of course, were voices of reason.

"Now wait a minute, guys. This might be just what we need to get our cost base back on track again. You know we've all been worried about the company's recent losses. Think about it. If the company goes down, we go with it. And I, for one, am too old to go out and hunt for a job. After twenty years, I like it fine right here. Let's give this a listen."

The consultant stood up front and waited for everyone to get the complaints out of their systems. He did have a baby face, which made him look younger than he may have been. His slight build compounded the effect, along with a shock of hair that fell on his forehead. Facial hair might have helped him look a little older, but he seemed unperturbed by it all. I was sure this was not the first time he had met with resistance. He stepped forward.

"Good morning. I think we can begin now. My name is John Matthews. I'm a consultant, and I'm here to share with you something that I think can help your company and one of the products that has put it in jeopardy. The methodology is called Value Analysis."

There were moans and sighs, and some eyes rolled.

"Maybe you know about it, or perhaps even tried it. But if you did, was it according to the Value Analysis job plan? That's what we're here to find out. Let's talk about it first, then do an exercise that will explain it better than I ever could, and then you be the judge. When we're all through, you tell me if you've heard it all before, and if you don't think it'll work."

"It worked for three guys at General Electric who were desperate during the Second World War: Lawrence Miles, Jerry Leftow and Harry Erlicher. There were shortages of all types of raw materials. They had to scramble to find different materials and parts to keep the production lines running and the company alive. On the way, not only did they often reduce their cost, but sometimes came up with a better quality product than before. That gave birth to what became known as Value Analysis."

"In those early days, Lawrence Miles would say, 'If I can't get the product, I've got to get the basic function.' Function and creativity, with an eye on cost, became the foundation of Miles' career. It won him awards and made him the father of Value Analysis, with worldwide acceptance."

Then John paused. It was dramatic. He looked at me and each of the men in the room and said, "I promise you that if you don't resist it, if you don't do 'business as usual' because it's comfortable, and if you follow the method through to its conclusion, you will be successful. But the best idea in the world is worthless if it's rejected out of hand or applied with half a heart. So give it a try. I think you'll be glad you did."

That did it. I could see that he at least had everyone's attention.

John turned to Mr. Davis. "Can you give us an intro, sir?"

Dean smiled and nodded. "Morning, all. I'm Dean Davis, Vice President of this company that gives us a place to come to and make a difference every day. So we have to take good care of this baby that's taken care of me, for example, for forty-seven years. We called this team together to solve one of our more serious customer issues, which you will hear about. Oh, yes," he said, "it's true we have customer problems like everyone else."

There were grunts and smiles around the table.

"So that you're aware of the pressure and urgency that prompted this gathering, let me tell you about our current position."

One guy near me turned to another and whispered, "Is it sleepy-bye time?"

The answer came back, "Not with that booming voice!"

But once Dean Davis began his recitation of the industry woes and how it impacted us, nobody could sleep. It was scary.

14

"For starters, we all know the economy is shot. No one can get financing to buy our airplanes. The Brazilians are stealing our market share; the Europeans are subsidized so much, they're almost giving airplanes away; the Mexicans are demanding offsets. That tells us we need to put more production work in Mexico, or they will buy from the Canadians. And now the Japanese have decided to get into the commercial airplane market. Gentlemen, and lady," he said as he bowed in my direction, "I don't have to tell you what they've done to the U.S. auto industry."

"Dean, do you mean to say we no longer have financial stability?" asked one of the attendees.

"I mean, my friend, that the analysts who follow our industry say that our rating has dropped, and we're in trouble. That brings us back to why we are here. We're not dead yet, and we will make damn sure we won't be. Improving value for our customers is the first step."

Uh-oh, did I make the wrong decision to come here? But I had no other offer on the table, plenty of debt from school, and I didn't want to wait to launch my career – not in these times. I'll have to stick with it and try to be more inventive and work harder, that's all. Maybe I can do some good here. I do have some great ideas - and so much more to learn.

"Some of you may be aware that UN Airways had a second rapid decompression in the last year. The blame is not on our doorstep in either case. The pilot in the first one failed to pressurize the cabin as he should have; the ground crew did not shut the aft cargo door in the proper way in the last instance. Both times, our check valves were stuck in the reverse flow direction and needed to be replaced."

"Whoa!" Bob said. "That valve was never designed to exceed 17 psi. Those incidents recorded over 20 psi. Of course our valves stuck." Bob's expressive hands helped to make his point.

"Relax, Bob. No one is calling your baby ugly. But maybe it could use a little alteration, because, one: even though it's selling well, it's selling at a loss, and that's unacceptable; and, two: come on, guys, this product failed our customers in the field, and that's totally unacceptable. That will reflect on every product we make and sell. Our reputation is everything. That's what this workshop is all about. It's to create value for our customers by increasing functions and reducing costs. It's to build quality with less expensive materials that will function even better, while it builds profit for us by bringing down our cost. That's right-brain thinking combined with left-brain logic. That's creativity before capital. That, people, is Value Analysis."

"Good luck with that!" whispered the same doubting Thomas a couple of seats away.

"Now let's get to it. Our consultant, here, can answer any questions you may have, or see me later. Sorry, I can't stay. I have a customer meeting. But let's meet again next week. I'll be anxious to hear about the design changes and financial improvements."

3

After Mr. Davis left, there was a lot of conversation that ranged all the way from depressed to determined. John waited for the group to settle down before he got up and addressed them.

"Look, everyone, I know this hasn't been the best news, but Dean's right. The reason for this workshop is to provide, as a first step, a methodology for this company to fight back to the position and reputation it enjoyed before. It will change the culture of the company. I know you will feel as positive about it as I do, once we get into it. So let's do it!"

As I listened to this man, I thought he should run for president. I knew I'd vote for him.

"First, I would like you all to go around the table and introduce yourselves."

There was immediate reaction.

"Oh, no!"

"I don't believe this."

"Is this necessary? We all know each other...well except you." He said while pointing at me.

"If you tell us who you are and what you do in the company," said John, "we will know who the go-to person is for specific issues." He looked around the room. "Since it's your part we're to examine, Bob, why don't we start with you?"

"Fine, but I don't think my parts need to be examined."

Everybody broke up. What are we? Still in college? *These guys were like fraternity brothers hazing a new pledge. I'm beginning to feel sorry for him.*

"Sorry. I'm Bob Green. I've been here thirty seven years. I'm the chief engineer for the Environmental Control Systems. My part, as you call it, the inlet check valve, is a crucial component of the environmental control system. It has already been redesigned and upgraded, John. We don't need a Lean production system," said Bob, as he swept his hand sideways and then he drew circles in the air. "And we sure don't need Quality Circles or Six Sigma or whatever they're calling basic statistics and the scientific method these days. I learned that in school forty years ago."

"Thanks, Bob. We'll come back to you on this in a minute. Who's next?"

"Hi, I'm Jake Evans, engineer with Environmental Control Systems. I'm Bob's extra pair of hands, and I believe Bob's right." Jake picked up a pencil and started tapping the eraser end of it against the table, trying to stay calm. "It's pretty hard to understand why we need to talk about a redesign of our inlet check valve, when our team already spent the past six months on that. Plus, we observe production and review supplier design ideas on a regular basis. I've been here only two years, but I'm proud of what we've achieved."

For some reason, he directed his gaze at me when he finished. *What was that about, I wondered?*

"You have to realize, Jake," John said, "that right now, the valve is selling at a loss. Our goal for this workshop is to increase the value of the product from the customer's point of view, and at the same time, turn a loss into a profit for the company. In an effort to do that, we'll apply the formula, Value is equal to Function divided by Cost, and we'll get into that shortly."

He turned to the next chair. "Good morning. I believe you're up now."

"Hold on a minute, John. How shortly? Because I still have a problem. I can't figure out how you picked this valve that has been a staple for thirty-five years, and is even better since it was redesigned in the last three months, out of three thousand parts in our portfolio." He emphasized these last words waving a pointing finger in the air.

Bob's passion for his job, this company and its products squirted out of him. As he spoke, his expressive hands made each word seem important. His gestures were like a second language. I smiled at that. I remembered people I'd heard described as unable to talk if they didn't use their hands. I'm convinced those people are profound thinkers and communicators, who leave little doubt about what they mean to say.

John didn't flinch. He seemed to understand Bob's frustration. "Bear with me, Bob. I promise I'll explain everything so that you'll have all the functions with which to work as a team. If there are too many digressions, it will distract from our agenda, and we might lose our focus." Let's finish this, okay? Please trust me." He nodded to the next man after Jake. "Go ahead. Please tell us who you are and what you do?"

"Yes, I'm Randy Jones from Procurement," he said as he pulled on his black handlebar mustache. I was asked to be here, because I buy all the purchased parts for the valve. I've been with this company seventeen years and counting."

"Excuse me, but don't you manufacture any of those parts here?" I asked. I glanced at Jake Evans. His arms were folded, and he shook his head as I spoke.

"No," Randy said, "we're not a fabrication site, and you would think there wouldn't be many parts to a small product like the valve. But it's made up of many purchased parts that we assemble. We buy the castings from Indiana, the reed components from Chicago, the hose clamps and other hardware from China, the gasket from somewhere in New England. Then we stamp the attach brackets in Kentucky, where some of the assembling is also done."

"Really!" I said. "Thank you."

"I assume I'm after you, Randy. Good morning.
Most of you know me," he said as he stood up and threw me
a side-glance. "I'm Chip Walters."

*Look at this guy! Slick! He must be at least six-feet-five, not
a hair out of place, dark suit, fancy tie, shiny Alarum lapel pin, sales
& marketing oozing from his pores.*

"I've been with the company thirty-five years, and I
look after our U.S. customer base. It's a good thing this
workshop was today or I wouldn't have been able to make it.
I fly out of here tomorrow morning on the corporate jet; I
have a meeting at UN Airways on Wednesday. But . . .uh . . .
I guess you didn't have to know that."

"Douglas McNabb, here, the assembly manager at
the Nashville facility."

It almost was not necessary for him to introduce
himself, with his fiery red hair and mustache. Just about
everybody in the company knew who "Red" was, I was told
later at coffee break.

"I'm responsible for the offload program to move
this assembly to our Ocotito, Mexico plant. But if we can
keep the assembly here, I won't have to lay off my second
shift. I came to see if there are things we could do to lower
the cost of this valve to make that happen. I sure hope so. So
does my second shift."

"I'm Leland . . . Leland Berk." His chair scraped on
the floor as he stood up, a little red-faced. "I work with the
design group. I create the CATIA models for EPIC, and I'm
here because whatever changes you guys come up with, I will
have to draft. The company and I have been together twenty
years, if you don't count our brief separation because of a
layoff, and because there was an offer I couldn't refuse."
Leland cleared his throat and sat down.

There were a few chuckles at that one.

Jake turned to me. "Okay, Princess, it's your turn."

There were smirks and more chuckles around the
room. *Pretty strange behavior for grown men and professionals, I*

thought. What are we, back in high school? I sensed the hair rising on the back of my neck. I know my blonde complexion must have been turning pink and my blue eyes into glowing coals because I could feel the steam come out of my ears. I rose out of my chair to my full five feet, six-inch height, and in a strong, decisive voice, I said, "First of all, gentlemen, my name is not Princess. And I'm quite sure, because of the gentlemen you all are, that no one here will ever address me by that name again." I let that sink into the silence for a moment.

Then, not to waste anymore time, I continued. "My name is Michelle Jamison. Today is my first day on the job, and I want to thank you all for making it so comfortable." A rash of throat clearing filled the air. "I graduated this month with a degree in mechanical engineering, and I'm to work in Environmental Control Systems." Managing a smile, I said, "I am excited to learn Value Analysis, and I want to become a useful member of the team. So I hope we can forget my gender, and just remember that I'm an engineer. Thank you." I took my seat.

"Uh, thank you, Michelle. And now, moving on . . . Bob, why don't you tell the team about this valve?"

"Yeah, sure, John. This is an inlet check valve, part of the environmental control system. It's not very big, but it does a big job. It has to satisfy both the environmental control system and the engine design team. I designed this valve in 1976 for the redesign of the wide-body aircraft. Since then, it has been a carryover for the narrow-body aircraft, as well as business jets. Now these units are on all passenger aircraft in production."

"There is one valve per engine, including the APU, and one valve per environmental control unit so there are anywhere from five to nine valves per plane. The rub has been that the unit costs us about $4,000.00 to produce, and we sell it for about $2,000.00."

Whoa, stapling two thousand dollar bills to every box is no way to stay in business.

"To use Dean's words, that can't be tolerated. It could kill us. That's why we made the changes three months ago, John."

"And when we reviewed all the products in the portfolio three weeks ago," said John, " to determine the part with the best potential for improvement through Value Methodology, another name for Value Analysis, by the way…"

"Wait a minute. I'm still trying to understand this. Out of three thousand products, the one you chose is one that has already been redesigned and is selling?"

"The thing is, when you changed the housing material from aluminum to pig iron, it reduced the cost, but then there was a weight problem – meaning more mass equals more cost for the airline customer. The current support brackets, I'm told, could not support the load in 9G load conditions. That required the secondary support structures group to increase the thickness of the support brackets. Plus there were the field failures in the last two rapid decompressions that you investigated."

"So how did you identify the valve for the project?"

"Okay, Bob, here it is. First of all, we knew we had to look for something that was high cost and steady future volume. Many practitioners use a method called Cost-Quantity Analysis. They take the unit cost of the product and multiply it by the forecasted annual volume. Then they 'Pareto' the results. A well-known Italian economist, Vilfredo Pareto, developed a curve known as Pareto's Law of Distribution. He died in 1923, but his famous theory lived on."

Bob interrupted, "Hang on. I didn't ask for a history lesson. We all know what a Pareto analysis is. Just tell us how this part was selected."

"Okay. The Cost-Quantity Analysis Pareto gave us our first short-list. 20% of the end item products in Alarum's portfolio had 80% of the costs. Then we added any products with negative margins. We rank this list looking at several criteria: potential financial benefits, business goals and probability of success. Although the inlet check valve was not at the top of the list, it was in the top ten and because of the recent customer issues Dean decided we would start there."

Bob interrupted again, "All you had to say was that Dean picked it."

John ignored him and continued. "Think, if you could take this basically great product and improve it to satisfy the customer and still make your profit! I don't know about you, but I would say that's an exciting challenge. And doesn't a little challenge now and then stir your soul?"

"Yeah, that's great, John, but . . .Well, I guess I was with you until now, but you mentioned satisfying the customer. Reducing costs doesn't say anything about the client's needs. Dean's concerned with bringing down the cost. So what about the quality and its ability to function to the client's satisfaction?"

"Ah, now you're getting it. That's where the Value Analysis Job Plan and the function phase, specifically, come in. That's why we didn't stop at cost analysis once we identified the project. Beginning with the customer's perceived value they acquire from goods and services, we applied the formula, value equals function divided by cost." John emphasized with big bold letters of the equation he drew on a flip chart.

"Bob, you know companies can't afford to have field failures like we had. Customers have a right to expect fair cost, quality and on-time delivery. The company that can't swing that loses its integrity, reputation and customer base. That's what's happening here right now. That's when we got you guys together before for your input, a cross-functional group to represent the points of view of all your departments." Chip added his customer perspective.

"We'll get into more of this later. I'm going to let you nourish yourselves with caffeine and sugar a.k.a. coffee and donuts while you digest what you've heard. The calories are at the back of the room. We'll resume in fifteen minutes."

John did not have to tell us twice. Chairs emptied quickly as several raced to the coffee urn.

As I strolled to the rear, I saw Jake coming toward me. Did he want to join me for coffee? I didn't think so.

4

"So you're the infamous Michelle Jamison."

"That's me. How did you know? Did you Google me?"

"Ha. No, but we were warned . . . I mean, told that you would be here."

"I hope you'll think that's a good thing, and not something to worry about."

"I'm not worried. Did I say I was worried? Why should I worry?

"I guess we'll be working together."

"So I understand. I'm Jake Evans."

"Yes, I know. As I said before, I hope to be able to contribute a great deal to you and to the team."

"I hope so, too. I guess we'll see about that, won't we?"

Jake turned and drifted away. I wasn't quite sure what to make of that. Was it a macho thing? That wouldn't make sense. Jake appeared to be about six feet three, with dark brown hair, dark eyes, and a body that looked as if he were at the gym every day. I wouldn't think anyone could challenge his ego.

I decided to go out to look for the ladies' room. When I came back, I thought I would talk with Bob before we sat down again. But I didn't have a chance. Jake brushed past me and beat me to it. I trust my instincts, and since he seemed in such a hurry to get there, I didn't want to join them. I guess I was right, because while Jake spoke, he kept nodding in my direction until Bob glanced my way, too. *Could you be a little more obvious, Jake? Is this what office politics is all about?*

For the moment, I pushed all that to the back of my mind as members of the group approached me. I was relieved that they accepted me into the fold in spite of my earlier speech.

"Excuse me . . . err, I'm Leland. He cleared his throat. It's nice to have you with us, Michelle," he said as he looked over his thick lenses and offered his hand.

"Thanks. I'm glad to be here." We shook, and I came away with my hand a little damp.

"Hi, I'm Randy. Welcome to the company."

"I remember, Randy, and thank you." *He must wax the ends of his mustache every day to keep it so perfectly curled. Do some women really find that attractive? Well I see at least one woman does based on that diamond studded ring on his finger.*

"I'm curious, how did you happen to go for engineering? I mean it's unusual for a woman to be interested in engineering."

I laughed. "Tell me about it! But I didn't mind being the only girl in all my classes. I grew up with four older brothers who always messed with cars and engines. Being the 'little sister,' I had to compete, and I came to love it. Later on, in order to keep up with them, I had to show them that I could solve mechanical problems that they couldn't. The competition was fierce with four egocentric brothers."

They all smiled and nodded.

"Okay, everyone, time to continue SAVE's Mod 1 Certification Value Analysis Workshop." John's voice rang out. "We have a lot to cover."

We shuffled back to our seats, some of us with our coffee cups still in our hands. It wasn't easy to adjust back into student mode after several days of celebrating my graduation.

After John counted noses, he said, "Well, now that the gang's all here, and before we dig in, let me begin by telling you that this workshop comes with a bonus. When we've completed our sessions here, you will all have the opportunity to sit for the AVS certification exam."

That was great news, as far as I was concerned. *The more CEU's I get, the better. Maybe this was a good decision, after all. I'll have room to grow here.* The rest of the crowd was not so happy.

"No way am I gonna waste more time and stay for a stupid test when I need to take care of work that I know must be piled high on my desk by now!" complained Bob. That frown was back again. His bushy eyebrows looked as if they had grown together.

"No one told me there would be a test," whined Doug. "In fact, no one told me about this workshop until almost the last minute. I think the quality manager was supposed to be here, anyway, and I took his place. Besides, I have to fly out the night before we're due to finish here. Bow-hunting season opens this weekend, and I need to check my deer stand."

"I'm afraid I'll have to miss it, too," Randy added. "We have commodity piece price reviews the day of the exam, and I have to be there."

"I should be back from my business trip by then, but I don't think it makes sense for me to sit for an exam after I've missed three full days, do you?"

"As a matter of fact, Chip, I do. And so does Dean, or he wouldn't have arranged this to begin with. This is a Mod 1 workshop, a one-time event that will help you learn a new methodology, save your company's reputation, your customer base and your company. And if that isn't enough, I believe you all are expected to be there for the exam."

"Now that I've said that, I invite you to open your minds to learn about something here that will engage you and leave you wanting to learn more. You've already heard Bob tell you a little about the part we've chosen and its history. Now we need to understand the customer's needs, the components and the processes for fabrication and assembly. Bob, if you would?"

"Can I have another donut?"

"Sure, if you hurry up and promise not to talk with your mouth full."

"Okay, then! Here's the scoop."

5

"The inlet check valve, this little part that we will work on, has its job cut out for it. The customer wants enough airflow to warm or cool the cabin. But when there is a slow decompression for landing, or a quick one as in the case of rapid decompression, the valve has to either restrict backflow or flow in the opposite direction, as needed. If this valve fails, we might stress the flow meters and compressors near the APU or other engines. The unit must be able to withstand one bar or one atmosphere of pressure. Typically, these units operate at 37,000 feet, which means at .75 bar. So now you have directional airflow and pressure requirements. Add to that the general rules of aerospace design, 'the lighter the better' and you'll have the perfect inlet check valve."

"It's too bad all the parts aren't made at the same plant where they are assembled. Vertical integration would be so much easier," John said.

"Don't we know it!" said Doug. "But we don't have that luxury. As Randy said, we buy them from everywhere. The assembly process isn't that difficult, though, and since we don't have to assemble more than about nineteen per day, our takt time is one per hour."

"That's a new word for me. What is takt time, Doug?" I asked.

"Oh, sorry. Takt time is the rate of customer demand that is expressed in seconds per unit, and because our volume is so low, we call it one hour. In other words, we must produce one valve every hour to satisfy our customers rate of demand."

"Share with the team how that's done, will you Doug?" asked John.

"My pleasure. First we make sure we have all the parts in place and ready to go. Then we assemble the reed sub-assembly into the lower housing. We place the gasket onto the lower housing, or body, and fasten it to the upper housing and its four fasteners to the support bracket. Then this assembly goes into a kit containing the hose clamps and support brackets, and the kit is packed in a returnable container in sets of six. We ship twice a week, once to each assembly plant. Orders for spares arrive about once a day, though."

"Are those handled the same way?" asked John.

"No, the usual order for those is one at a time. And even though we lose money on the production valve, we make money on the spares, because, as a rule, there needs to be a replacement during 'D' checks. We wrap the spares in bubble wrap, place them in cardboard boxes, and ship them Overnight Next Day Air. The carrier we use depends on where they're to be shipped."

"Thank you, Doug. Now, if any of you have further questions about this, you know the man with the answers."

Leland leaned over and whispered to me, "Listen, Michelle, if you need help with anything, I'll be happy to do what I can. I remember when I was brand new. I know learning the language is not easy. And sometimes these guys speak in acronyms."

"That's so nice of you. I'm sure I'll need all the help I can get."`

He handed me a piece of paper. "Here's my phone extension," he said. "Give me a buzz if you have a problem."

"Okay. Thanks."

"Care to share, Leland?" asked John.

"Uh, no. Just explained something to Michelle," he said. He blushed a light pink.

"Ha! And you really think that will help? Lot's of luck!" Jake sneered.

What is the matter with that guy!?

My mind drifted for a minute to try to put things into perspective. I expected that there might be some reaction when I entered a male domain, but Jake seemed to feel it was a personal threat. I'm sure the fact that I was assigned to his department had something to do with it. If he knew me, though, he'd realize I wasn't after his position, that all I wanted was to learn and do a good job for the company. If, of course, my presence helps to open up a corner of the industry for women, that's all right too. But I hope everyone here understands that's not my goal. How do I prove myself? Jake would never believe me. I'll have to think of a plan that will change his mind, or this job could become miserable.

"May we continue now?" John asked.

Leland smiled. "You may."

"Then get ready for the next adventure, folks, the essence of Value Analysis -- Function. We'll begin with Random Function Identification. This is the fun part. Think of it as a lab class. You'll need to put on your thinking caps, as well. What is Value Analysis all about? It's about thinking in functions. This is how we'll begin our analysis. Is everyone ready?"

"Bring it on!"

"I have no other plans at the moment."

"Fill my dance card."

John looked down and slowly shook his head.

6

"When I learn something new," said John, I like to start with a dictionary, even if I think I know the definition. Don't laugh, because you might be surprised at what you can sometimes find there. In this case, however, when I looked up 'function' it told me what I expected. It said, 'the purpose for which something is designed'.

"But Value Engineering goes one step further to describe what the parts do to make that something work. It becomes a functional description. If you put an active verb together with a noun you can measure or quantify, you have a 'work function', which you can later relate to cost.

For example, a function of a coffee cup is to 'contain liquid'; the function of an electric bulb is to 'emit light'. The simple two-word descriptions allow you to bypass the technical and design jargon, so that all the team members, pulled from a cross-section of the company, understand. It frees you to focus on the job at hand. So it makes sense to first list all the work functions of each component part to begin Random Function Identification, but to always keep in mind that the focus is on the customer's needs. That is considered the foundation of Value Analysis."

"Since this is a 'lab' session, we won't use the valve just yet; we will use a mousetrap, instead, to illustrate this step. As you can see, you are about to be passed one, now."

"Why a mousetrap, of all things? I asked. "How does that relate?"

"This will demonstrate, Michelle, that the Value Analysis process can be applied to everything. The methodology involves function, and everything has a function. This is a simple tangible example everyone is familiar with and it does not require any technical expertise. Who knows, maybe we can build a better mousetrap that will draw more satisfied customers?" John quipped as he passed out sheets with active verbs and measureable nouns.

That prompted a few smiles.

"Examine it. Think about it for a moment, and we'll start with simple components of the mousetrap. First, let's list all the functions of this fastener. Michelle, will you lead the group on this phase, please?"

The expression on Jake's face said that he wasn't happy. It was a "why didn't he pick me" kind of face.

I didn't expect to be asked. My smile faded. I must have looked like a deer frozen in headlights, because John said, "Come on, now, I'm sure you've done this kind of thing before, and not long ago, either. Don't worry. Jake won't say anything unless he has something useful to contribute. Right Jake?"

"No sir . . . I mean, that's right."

"Well, then . . . What are the functions of this fastener?" I moved to the flip chart that was already set up in the room. John handed me the marker.

Each man in his turn sized up the mousetrap with a discerning eye. The responses were slow at first, and then they came rapid-fire. I wrote them down as they were called out, while John wrote them on post-it-notes.

"A fastener connects parts."

"It prevents corrosion, because it has a zinc oxide finish."

"Creates torque."

"Good," said John. "What else?"

Bob looked at the trap; he turned it in all directions. Silence filled the room. I shifted from one foot to the other, my marker poised, while I waited for the next shout-out, when . . .SNAP! All heads turned in the direction of the sound. There sat Bob sucking on his finger where the trap's striker bar had caught it.

"Well, thanks to Bob, we know the trap still works," John said, amid team laughter and shaking heads.

"It increases production," said Bob, holding the tip of his injured index finger to his mouth.

"What?"

"I said that the fastener increases production."

"Thank you. I can understand you better when your finger isn't in your mouth."

"Very funny!"

"So how can a fastener do that?"

"Well, there are several fasteners, but they all have the same Phillip's head. That makes it easier for operators to assemble, and that creates a faster production line. Many of our own products are put together with multiple fastener types. It becomes difficult to keep them separated on a production bench and causes clutter with all the different tools."

"Wow," said John, "when you stop to think how many functions a simple screw has . . . huh! Okay, let's move on to another component, the wooden base. Let's see what that does. Ready Michelle?"

"All set."

"It holds all the components together -- it holds parts," someone called out.

"And it stores setting instructions."

"Contains weight."

"It absorbs force."

"Limits motion," came from Randy.

John stopped writing. "Now there's one for you. How does it manage that?

"If the wooden base weren't there, the striker bar would rotate 360 degrees."

"Very good, Randy. What else?"

The room was quiet. You could almost hear the mental wheels turn.

"Anybody?" John looked around the table.

"It defines space."

"Very good. You did well, team, but we're not quite through."

"When we've designed that new mousetrap, we will want customers, right? There's another type of function to consider, the 'sell function'. Now remember, in Value Methodology, the purpose of the part and the client's needs are the main factors to determine basic function. I can't stress that enough. Sell functions contribute little to that; they're more concerned with appeal, and they cost a lot more. Although it can sometimes be what sells the customer, purpose and need will more often trump appeal in industrial products. Because Value Methodology identifies the costs of the two functions separately, it makes it a lot easier to determine a function that is unnecessary and can be eliminated or reduced in cost."

"You will still use the same two-word designation system to identify the sell function as you did with the basic, but this time with a passive verb and less-measureable noun. For example: 'improves product' or 'enhances appearance'. Now think about how you would apply a sell function to the mousetrap's wooden base."

"We'll let you off the flip chart for that one, Michelle. Thank you. How about you, Jake? Will you help us out?"

"Who, me?'

"Yes, that would be great."

The look Jake gave me as he passed me on the way up to the chart, I wouldn't give to my worst enemy. *What a baby!*

The sell function words for the base of the mousetrap took a little more thought but we came up with a few.

I said, "The base provides form."

"Displays brand," came from Leland.

"Facilitates setting," added Randy.

"Good. You all seem to have the idea. Any questions about where we're going with this? No?" John looked at his watch. "Okay then. Time for lunch, and when we come back in, say, forty-five minutes, we still have two functions to look at before we sink our teeth into the real thing. Thank you, Jake."

"I'm for that," said Doug, on the way out. "My stomach is growling."

"Good thought! I'm ready for that, too," piped Randy.

Chip was the first one to reach the door. He turned around. "Hey, why don't we all go out together? There's this place I know a couple of blocks away. It's fast, and the food is good. You should come, too, John, but only if you don't talk shop -- or should I say 'workshop'?"

"Fine." He laughed. "I'd like that."

Bob hung back and hemmed and hawed.

"Come on, Bob. Give it a rest. You'd never make it to the office, take care of whatever is lurking on your desk, grab a bite and make it back here in forty-five minutes."

There was a big sigh from Bob. "I give up. You're right," he said.

"Last one out, shut the door," yelled John.

7

You couldn't tell from the windowless room we'd been meeting in that it was a bright, sunny day. I suppose the purpose of that was to keep the students from being distracted. It felt good to feel the warm breeze and to breathe fresh air again.

One of my brothers used to tell me my head cleared on a windy day because the wind went in one ear and out the other with nothing to stop it in between. *Thanks, brother Brian! That's the same brother that told me salt and lemon juice would help my skinned knee.* How strange when memories pop up at unexpected moments.

In front of the college building, patches of flowers and new-mown grassy areas gave off a heady scent. I noticed a wooden bench in the center, begging to be occupied by someone with a good book.

Since it was a short two-block walk to the restaurant, none of us felt the need for cars on such a nice day. Bob fell into step beside me on the way.

"Well, Michelle, what do you think?"

"What do I think? I'm thrilled. I'm where I wanted to be. I feel as if I can reach my career goals here."

"Michelle, since we will be working together, I have to ask you something now -- and please be straight with me. Do those goals mean you intend to move up as fast as you can, no matter who's in your way?"

I stopped dead in my tracks. "Bob, what made you ask a question like that? That's about the farthest thing from my mind that I could imagine!"

"Someone suggested you might be thinking along those lines, and I had to clear the air before we went any further."

"Who? This is my first day. No one even knows me here." *He didn't have to tell me who it was.* "All I can say is that I have so much to learn, like Value Analysis. And I am so excited to have this opportunity."

"Let's just say someone thought it might be a possibility."

"Bob, please believe me when I tell you that my only goal is to become the best engineer I can be, and I know that will take some time."

"I'm glad to hear you say that, Michelle, and we'll do our best to help you reach that goal. Welcome to the club."

"Thank you. Now I'm really hungry."

We were almost at the restaurant when Chip called out, "Hey, look at this! They've set up an outdoor eating area. That's new since the last time I was here. Very nice. Alfresco okay?"

"Yeah, cool." said Jake.

"Who wants to dine alfresco?" asked Chip

Bob said, "Sounds good."

Everyone agreed. We didn't mind the brief wait while they put two tables together to accommodate all of us. I was about to sit down, but hesitated when I saw a familiar figure a short distance away -- a woman who looked a lot like Sally. I thought I would go over to say hello, but then I remembered Sally probably wasn't even here yet. It was too soon after she'd been hospitalized. She wouldn't have traveled right away, if at all.

"Is something the matter?" Bob asked.

"No, I thought I saw someone I knew, but it couldn't be." I dismissed the idea and took my seat.

As the waitress came out to take our orders, the smell of comfort food and strong coffee hit me through the open door and woke up my taste buds. I was more than ready for lunch.

"Hello, my name is Marie. What can I get for you?"

We told her we were on a short leash, and she made a special effort for us. That was a good thing, because I might have taken a bite out of the table. Our orders went in and came out fast. There wasn't anything gourmet -- hamburgers with fries, but they were good, and even better if you're starved.

"How did you find this diner, Chip?" Jake asked. "It's not bad."

"My kids and I sometimes grabbed a quick bite here after practice. The park district is right around the corner."

With the weather cooperating, it was pleasant to sit there and eat outdoors. We were protected from cars that drove by and parkers alongside the restaurant. Small trees had been planted in open squares in the sidewalk near the curb, spaced a few feet apart. One of them was in front of our table. A low wrought iron fence separated us from pedestrians. There was a whiff of air, and just enough sun filtered through the trees to cheer us, but keep us cool.

That silence that's known to happen in small gatherings about every sixty minutes or so took over as everyone cleaned their plates.

My lunch partner, who sat on my right, gave me a nudge. "Hey, Michelle, I heard you had a rough flight into Chicago yesterday. Glad to hear you're okay. What happened there, do you know?"

"No, I don't, Chip, other than the fact that we had two rapid decompressions, one right after the other. I haven't had time to look into it, but I intend to research it. I know they've found ways to prevent some of it over the years, but I can't help but feel that there is more to be done."

"Like I mentioned in the workshop, I'm supposed to fly out Wednesday. I fly all the time, and I never had anything like that happen."

" Odds are, you won't. Don't worry. Keep your seat belt buckled. You'll be fine."

"Dean told me our valves jammed."

"Is that why you are going to the customer tomorrow?"

"All right, everybody. Sorry, but back to work," John's voice rang out above the chatter.

"I knew we shouldn't have invited him," somebody said. "Could we move the workshop over here?"

John smiled. "I'll put that in the suggestion box. Oh wait we don't have a suggestion box. So...No!"

Back in our student seats again, I sensed the gang was more interested in the workshop now than they were at first. I was glad, because it made me feel that I would have my colleagues' support and would be able to learn more.

John took his place at the front of the room. I was curious to find out what was next.

8

"Welcome back, y'all," John said. He paused and let his gaze fall on everyone; we looked back at him with anticipation.

"As we went through this morning's session," he said, "I watched you absorb the material we covered, each in your own way. Some of you took copious notes, while you visual learners took it all in, confident you would retain it very well. But however you process new information, I think it's important to review the difference between the systems you've used in the past and what you've learned about Value Analysis this morning. Jake, in a few words, can you remind us what Lean is?"

"Yeah . . . uh . . .you reduce Lead Time by getting rid of waste."

"And what about Six Sigma, Bob?"

"That's when we reduce variability through the DMAIC approach."

"Right. Now why is Value Analysis different? Anybody?

"Michelle. I noticed you're one of the note-takers. How is VA different from the other programs?"

"I understand it focuses on an increase in value from the customer's point of view, because it reduces costs and/or increases functionality."

"Good description. So what you said, Michelle, is that Value Analysis complements the other traditional programs, but is separate from them at the same time."

"I guess I did."

"Great," John said. "We're almost there. Now I want to introduce you to two more functions that help make Value Analysis the powerful tool that it is."

"Excuse me, John, will we be able to start on the part today?"

"Maybe, Randy. I think so. We do have Dean's deadline to keep in mind. But I want to be sure you all understand everything, first, and then we'll jump in. Plus this may be on the Mod 1 certification exam."

"If I haven't etched it in your minds, let me say again that the basic function is concerned with the specific, immediate needs of the client. It's what the product or part is made to do. This next function, higher order, is what the basic function exists to satisfy; it's what makes the basic function necessary."

"We can use an aircraft's inlet check valve as an example. We know that its basic function is to control airflow, right? The higher order function in this case, then, must be to stabilize the environment. Note that logic and order are vital ingredients throughout the VA recipe. You'll see what I mean further on."

"Now take a deep breath, because our next ride will take us through a function system that gets down to the nitty-gritty and ties it all together. Then you'll have the intellectual and creative tools you'll need to answer the question, 'How do we give our customers more value and our company a new reputation?'

"It's a process called FAST diagramming, developed by Charles W. Bytheway of the Sperry Rand Corporation. Have you heard of it? Don't get too excited. FAST diagramming has nothing to do with speed. It's an acronym for Function Analysis System Technique. It's been called the most powerful technique used in the Value Methodology, and was Bytheway's contribution to the stimulation of creative thinking. We can all use some of that, right? As you might guess, you were not the first engineers to be introduced to this system. That honor belonged to members of the National Conference of the Society of Value Engineers, in 1965."

"FAST builds on the same verb/noun rules that apply to the component parts of the mousetrap you practiced with earlier. It is different from random function identification. It is a visual logic system."

"You mean because of the diagramming?" asked Leland

"That's part of it," said John. "I thought you might pick up on that, Leland. But there's much more. It shows how the functions relate to each other and may support each other to form a system. In that way, it helps point out any functions that may be missing. Remember when you worked with the other functions, you analyzed each part separately? FAST Diagramming analyzes a system as a whole, not just its parts. That's the main difference between the two. But it also discerns basic functions from sell functions and other secondary functions."

"Furthermore, FAST Diagramming is interactive. The whole team gets involved in discussion. Logic, as I mentioned before, is an important factor as you decide on the nouns and verbs to build the diagram. Without logic and a lot of collaboration, you won't be able to see how things connect. Discussion will allow ideas to flow. Everybody will get to voice their view, increase their knowledge and be part of the final decision based on consensus. Only then is a FAST Diagram complete."

"Any questions so far? Yes, Randy."

"Where does the diagramming come in, and how much of it is there?"

"The diagrams are used throughout the process, and as the diagrams increase and expand with all the elements of the project in it, a whole system is defined and analyzed. This is how it works:

"As an example, draw two small oblong blocks adjacent to each other in your notes. Okay? Now, print 'HOW' above the left box with an arrow pointing to the right; above the right box, print 'WHY' with an arrow pointing to the left. Then draw a single line between the two boxes at the center outside edge. That's your basic structure."

"For now, let's say our subject is the inlet check valve again, and you've already discussed the functions. Start from the left, the 'HOW' side, to focus on your goal. We'll begin in this case with the higher order, which would be 'Stabilize Environment'. But can anyone tell me why we cannot use the noun, 'environment' in the diagram? How about you, Michelle?"

"Because it's not measurable or quantifiable?"

"Correct. And is there another word we can use, instead?"

The computer in my head whirred around. Just as he was ready to move off to someone else, I said, "Area. That's measurable."

"Good for you, Michelle. The higher order function, then, 'Stabilize Area', can be placed on the far left of the chart. Applying logic, the next two-word description will tell you how that's done. 'Control fluid' will be the next box on the HOW side, and is the basic function. The box following might read 'Adjusts Flow'. It's important, team, you understand that once you have decided on the basic function, it cannot be changed, since how to accomplish that function and all the other functions on the right will be affected."

"To continue, as you expand your diagram, keep going from the 'HOW' direction toward the right, or WHY. That's how you will catch every function process and avoid gaps. However, if your team approves the answers, you can do your building from either end as well, as long as it satisfies logic."

"From the start, you'll begin to see the functions' dependence on each other to create a system. To test the logic of your 'HOW' findings, read from the 'WHY' direction toward the left. That reverse logic as you read it will tell you if your selected functions have been well described and identified. If not, the functions won't read in a logical manner from right to left, as they do from left to right.

"You may also extend your boxes downward to express supporting functions, for example: a line drawn connecting a box below to the function above, because it is caused by it or happens at the same time. You are then using the 'WHEN' logic."

"How am I doing so far? Was I clear? Any questions, so I can confuse you more?"

"Yes, John. How long should the FAST diagramming session be?" asked Randy. Is there a length of time when we stop discussions and start diagramming?"

"Good question, but not an easy answer," said John. "You'll know when it's time when all the functions have been discussed and everyone agrees that the Technical FAST diagram reflects the system we are working on."

"Once you begin to work with this, I don't think you'll have a problem. But ask me anything at any time. I'll be glad to help you. Combined with everything else you've learned about Value Analysis, you should have the picture of what separates the Value Analysis methodology from all the other continuous improvement processes. Now you have a foundation on which to build a new model for our product . . . excuse me, Bob's part, the inlet check valve."

Bob waved from his seat at the table.

"And we're going to do that when you get back from your break. Stretch your legs and your minds, and I'll see you in ten."

9

I paid close attention all through the workshop proceedings, taking the copious notes that John talked about earlier. This was a full, busy day, with not much time to think about anything else. But always at the back of my mind was the memory of the flight disaster that I experienced on my way to Chicago, and my equally burning need to find out what caused it. Since after business hours would be too late to reach anyone at the airline, I had to make use of these ten minutes to at least begin to search for answers, my own answers, even though it was only last night that the disaster had occurred.

I managed to slip out unnoticed as soon as we were dismissed. I saw someone in the hall who looked as if she knew the building, and asked where the best place would be to make a quiet phone call. She pointed to someone's office and said, "Why don't you go in there. She's not in today. I'm sure she wouldn't mind."

"Thank you. That helps. I am in a hurry."

I sat down at the desk, but I decided not to use the phone there, and grabbed my cell phone, instead. "Operator? May I have the number for UN Airlines please? . . . Pardon me? . . . No, not reservations. Is there a Customer Relations Department number? . . . You can call the number for me? Thank you."

I got up and paced the floor a couple of times; then I sat down again and began tapping my foot. There were about six rings before they answered, and I was having kittens. It began to seem like it would take longer than I thought. I had to get back to the meeting. At last someone picked up."

"Hello. My name is Michelle Jamison. I was a passenger on Flight 465 from Sarasota, Florida to Chicago. You know, the flight that had to emergency land in Orlando yesterday? I know it's a bit soon, but is there any information about what caused the decompression? I'm an engineer. I'm anxious to know, so that I can study a similar situation. . . Oh, they don't know yet? . . . Of course not. What was I thinking! The National Transportation Safety Board is still investigating, aren't they? Do you have any idea how long it might take? . . . Yes, I guess these things do sometimes take a while...but you can't give me any information?...somebody is already suing the airline?...damned lawyers!"

I didn't move right away. Remembering that terror in the sky pinned me to the seat. "Oh, my God," I said, suddenly coming to. I jumped up and ran down the hall.

"It's nice of you to join us, Michelle. We missed you," John said.

"I'm so sorry. I had to make a call."

Of course, there was a snicker from Jake's chair. I'm certain he couldn't resist.

"No worries. In your absence the group came up with a team name: BMW, Bob and the Micro Waves. It won out over Michelle and the Velvet Lapelles."

"Thank goodness!"

"Okay," John said, "where were we?"

I no sooner took my seat, than heavy footsteps sounded nearby and stopped outside our door.

"Gee, if I didn't know better, I'd think that was Dean," said Bob. "For a trim guy, he sounds like a five-ton press operating at capacity. There couldn't be another one like him."

Everyone watched as the door opened, and in walked Mr. Davis. He looked tired.

"Good afternoon, team. How's it going?"

I thought the room was too small for his voice. I wondered if there was a switch that could turn down the volume. The group muttered their "good afternoon's" and "fine's" and waited for him to speak.

"This is a surprise." John lied.

"Sorry to break in on you like this," Dean blared. "My meeting ended earlier than I expected. There were a couple of unhappy phone calls for me when I got back. That seems to be a trend these days. I'll be straight with you. This little workshop is even more important than I indicated earlier. It's urgent that we get to the design work ASAP. We've got to move fast. I know you weren't happy about it when you started. How do you all feel about it now that you've had some training?"

"It's good, Dean."

"It's what we needed."

"I like the challenge."

What a bunch of 'Yes men.' They have been virtually kicking and screaming all day.

"Good. Then I hope you won't mind if I sit in on the rest of this today. I haven't done one of these before, and I'd like to get a sense of it. Pretend I'm not here."

They'll be on their best behavior now.

10

Pretend he's not here? He is here. He's the vice president of the company? It was like my dad chaperoning my junior high dance all over again. Pretend I'm not here he said. Yeah right!

How do you pretend the man being groomed to be the next CEO is not sitting behind you? But John was a professional. "We could always use some help," he said.

"How about the valve today, John?" Leland asked.

"I had that in mind. You guys did such a great job on the mousetrap, using the two-word Random Function Identification process. You remember all that, right? Let's show Dean what you can do with the real thing. Game on! This is the first step. Who will take over the flip chart? Leland, how about you?"

Leland hoisted himself out of the chair. He was about five feet ten when he stood up. "Sure," he said. A flush on his cheeks told me he didn't like to have a spotlight focused on him. He took off his glasses and wiped them on the bottom of his plaid shirt. Worn outside his trousers, the shirt made him seem heavier than his medium build. He put the glasses back on and took his place, marker in hand. He was a little shy, maybe, but he impressed me as someone who could be counted on.

I noticed that John had a fresh supply of post-its. Wow! Did he expect to use them all? The room went quiet. It was as if everyone waited for the starting gun to go off. All that remained was to determine which part of the valve we would address first. The mighty Bob Green rose to his feet and said, "Why don't we start with the fasteners, like we did before? That ought to get the ball rolling."

I could swear the room temperature went up a few
degrees, and the shout-outs began much as before, but with
more enthusiasm:

"Connects parts."

"It prevents corrosion."

"Creates torque."

And the list went on until the next part of the valve
was scrutinized and broken down into two-word functions.
There were many. And many duplicates.

Then in the midst of that frenzy, I saw John glanced
at his watch, and he called a halt to the day. I didn't think
anyone expected that.

"But we're not through yet. There are still some parts
to work on," said Randy.

"I know, and I hate to have you stop, but I think
you've got it down now. It's almost time to close, anyway, so
we'll quit a little early. We can make this up tomorrow, since
Dean asked me to tell you to come here for an early start,
instead of the office. Right Dean?"

"We're fighting time, folks. Which means Chip your
customer trip has been postponed. And Randy your deer
stand will be fine until Saturday. I expect each and every one
of you to make this project your priority. Any questions?"

"No questions?" thankfully John broke the silence,
"I'd like you to leave here anxious for more, instead of being
tired of it all."

"I don't believe it!" said Bob. He threw up his
hands in that familiar gesture. "I'm sure all that work on my
desk has children by now!" He stomped out, pouting.

Dean couldn't help but smile. "That's our Bob."

"Thank you for your patience, everyone. Wait until
you see what tomorrow will bring. If you liked today, you'll
love tomorrow. Have a good night," John said, and winked at
Dean. The wink said, "Thanks for coming and showing them
that this means something."

50

11

It was after 5:00 by the time we had gone through the Random Function Identification phase for the day. When I looked around, I noticed Dean was involved in conversation. We were all tired, but we were looking forward to successfully completing this project. We were invested in each other's future, and we knew it.

When I got ready to leave, I thanked everybody as if I were a guest at a party. I told them that it was nice to meet them, and that I would look forward to working with them, and I meant it. I couldn't have been more pleased with the choice of employment I had made.

I had one foot out the door, when Dean Davis called my name. I chuckled to myself, because with his voice, there was no way I couldn't hear him over the chatter.

"Mr. Davis. You were talking with John. I didn't want to disturb you."

"Everyone else calls me Dean. We're very informal here, Michelle. How was your first day?"

"It felt like my first week, but I loved it. I'm happy to be here, Dean."

"That's good, because we're happy to have you. Do you have a ride back to your car?"

"It's not far. I was going to walk."

"Well, come on. I'll drive you." We climbed in and headed for the office. "That would be nice. Thank you."

"Tell me, what did you think about the Value Analysis workshop?"

"I thought it was interesting. I had attended a SAVE chapter meeting last semester. What a mind it took to develop a process like that to revolutionize thinking. I know it must have taken an awful lot to tear people away from the traditional wisdom back then. But you said this was rather new to you, too. What did you think, Dean?"

"You're right. That was quite a demonstration. I was impressed, too. Frankly, though, I do not see where this is leading and how describing everything in two-word functions is going to give us the breakthrough we need. The fact we are selling at a loss is bad but the fact that we have a very unhappy long-term customer is worse. Confidentially, we know they are looking for a new supplier for our valves. This is a goodwill effort to proof to them we are serious about improving the quality of our products."

"Say, enough business. And if the union hears me talking shop after hours I'll find myself in front of those bastards at the NLRB."

"NLRB?"

"Never mind that...I heard you had a terrible time on your way into Chicago yesterday. I'm glad you weren't hurt."

"It was frightening. But I'm determined to find out what caused it, and to do something about it. You know, as an engineer, I feel it's almost an obligation."

He turned and looked at me without saying anything.

"Oh, don't worry. I won't take any time away from the company. But wouldn't it be great if, after we've solved our current problems, we could develop a team to figure out how to cut down on the occurrence of some of these decompressions?"

"Hold on to those thoughts, Michelle. Those are the kinds of ideas that keep the world humming."

As we rolled into the company's parking lot, I said, "Thank you for the lift, Dean. Do you mind if I go back to my office for a minute? There's something I'd like to check on my computer."

"No, I don't mind, but don't stay long. The cleaning crew will be coming by soon, and you might be in their way."

"I won't, and thank you for hiring me and giving me this chance."

"You're welcome. I think we made the right choice."

"I think I did, too. Good night."

"We'll see you tomorrow," Dean said as he drove away.

The glass doors in the front were still open. I guessed they would be until the crew was finished. It was an impressive sight to walk into those corporate halls. Everything was marble, glass and stainless steel. It screamed of modern thinking and innovation.

I went down the hall; to my right was my cubicle. My luck, Jake's cubicle was right next to mine. I was glad to see he wasn't there.

I sat down at my desk and looked around. Here, too, furnishings were simple, but sleek. Most of the pictures on the wall were airplanes in various stages of takeoff and flight. I couldn't believe I was here at last.

I rolled my chair to the computer and turned it on. I wanted to see if the internet had any further information for me. There was one email message. Who knows my email? Strange. Who knew I was here? I hesitated; I didn't recognize the address. I hovered my mouse over it, and then I clicked.

Sally? Where did she get my address?

"Hello Michelle," she wrote. "I bet you're surprised. It was hard to find you. But I had to. You let me down. You told me you'd take care of me on that plane, but you didn't. You just looked out for yourself, and I'll never forgive you for that. I didn't want to say anything, but then I decided you deserved to know. I'll never let you forget. Your fellow traveler, Sally."

My heart was pounding, and a chill went down my spine. My hand was frozen on the mouse.

I heard vacuum cleaners and people in the halls. That meant the cleaning crew. I pulled myself together, picked up my things and left in a state of disbelief. I hoped the fresh air outside would clear my head.

I got into my car . . . not really mine. It was my mom's old car. I would have to wait for a few paychecks to buy my own. I tried to collect myself. It took several minutes until my breathing was normal. Then, being the rational person I've always been, I decided she probably had to get that out of her system, and I would never hear from her again. That would be too bazaar.

I reached for my phone to try to talk to someone again about the plane event. How silly of me. There was no one to call until the NTSB determined the cause. And who would tell me anything anyway? Sounds like some passengers already lawyered up. Maybe the internet would provide some general information as to the possibilities, though, to formulate some theories. That would be a start, anyway. *Note to myself: Stop at the library and go on line to look up known cases of airplane decompressions.* Maybe someone could help with that at work, but only during off-hours.

Okay, Michelle, put the key in the ignition and get home before something else happens.

I started to turn the key, there was a knock on my window. I looked up. It was Jake.

12

Mom met me at the door, not yet used to having me home for dinner. Dad came next with the hugs and kisses. Wonderful smells flowed from the kitchen, one of the things I missed at school. Top Ramen only tastes good when you are really hungry. I won't be missing that about school!

"Hey, family, I love you, too, but I can't get through the door!"

We all laughed. They backed off and I slid between the two of them directly to the kitchen.

"Are you two going to spoil me like this next week?"

"I doubt it," Dad said," so enjoy it while ya' got it."

"That's not fair. What kind of parents are you?"

We sat down to a meal of the best chicken riganati I've ever tasted. We could cut the chicken with a spoon, and I could have made a meal on the sauce alone. Mom served it with garlic asparagus, corn infused rice cakes and a caprese salad. It was never like that down at old Embry-Riddle.

They allowed me enough time to get some food into me, before Mom asked the question, "So tell us, how was your first day?"

I decided not to mention Sally or Jake. At least not yet. I didn't want them to worry.

"I'm tired. I have to admit, it was a lot to take in at one time. And then, of course, there's that thing about tension and nervousness, and not sure what to expect in a brand new environment. We were in a meeting all day, Mom, about a new way to analyze a product."

"You mean Value Analysis?" asked Dad.

"How did you know?"

"Well, it's not that new, and I wasn't always retired, you know. I still have my original Mod 1 notebook."

"Really? You do?"

Mom disappeared into the kitchen. I heard the water run, and the clink of dishes, and the refrigerator door when she put the food away. The wonderful aromas lingered.

"Yes! You liked it, right? " Dad asked.

"Dad, I loved it! Except . . ."

"Except what? Is something wrong?"

"Well, there's this man." *Oops I wasn't going to say anything.*

"Did he bother you?"

"Not exactly, not the way you think."

"Then what?"

"He's a man who's very insecure, Dad. I was placed in the same department, and I think he views me as a threat to his position and status. I know I have to do something to change his perception, but I'm not sure what."

"Has he done anything?"

"He's just hostile. He derided me at the meeting, suggested that he didn't think I was worth anything, and he tried to convince our boss that I intended to step on people to get to the top. Then as I was about to drive out of the parking lot, he knocked on my window to say he hoped I wouldn't be up all night trying to understand everything in case it was too much for me. Then he said, "Have a nice night.""

"But, Princess, you've only been there one day!" *Only Dad can call me Princess.*

"Exactly! He'll make my life miserable, if I let him. What am I going to do?"

"Hmm." Dad thought a minute, then he said, "Don't let him."

"What do you mean?"

"Michelle, make him your ally, your partner. Are there any other projects besides the one you had the meeting for today?"

"That's the one we're supposed to focus on, but I suppose there are others. After all, we can't just shut down for this. And then there's my own idea to find out what caused the air tragedy I was in, and do some research on that."

"Then you have a lot of options. Pick one, and ask him to help you with it, because 'you have so much more experience with these things than I do, and our boss would be impressed that you knew so much and wanted to help me'. Make him your mentor instead of your enemy."

"Dad, you're a genius!" I got up and kissed him smack on his forehead.

"I could have told you that," came the voice from the kitchen. Mom didn't miss a thing.

13

When I woke up the next morning, I gulped down a quick breakfast and took a cup of coffee-to-go in the car with me, much to Mom's disappointment. Dad gave me a thumbs-up as I raced out the door. I itched to get to that meeting to start the real work. I felt I could focus better, too, now that I had a handle on how to deal with Jake if it got too bad.

I was early, so I went on to the meeting room and looked over my notes while I finished my coffee. No one else was there. My phone rang. Oh! Darn! I thought I had turned it off!

"Hello? Who is this? . . . Sally? What do you want? How did you get my number? . . . You what? You called my parents and told them you were a friend from college? How dare you, Sally! . . .Oh, you just wanted to remind me you're here? Listen, don't ever call them again, don't call this number, and don't send me any more emails. Hello? Hello? Sally . . ."

I was stunned. I didn't expect to hear from her again. I became aware of an eerie sense of danger that I've never experienced before. I know I said I would figure it out if it came to this, but what do I do now?

Then the door opened. Jake walked in. Perfect. My day was complete, and it hadn't even started yet.

"Good morning," he said. "I see you got here ahead of me. Did you think you'd make points for being first?"

"What? Jake, what are you talking about? I just happened to get here early. It wasn't planned."

"Sure, sure. Well, I'm glad you're here, because there's something I wanted to say to you. I think, except for Bob, you should let me do most of the talking at meetings from now on, so you don't embarrass the department. After all, you're still so new."

I opened my mouth, but nothing came out. It might have been shock. But that wore off in a second, about the time John entered. Jake was lucky, because whatever I would have said, I might have regretted.

"Well, good morning, you early birds." He took one look at our faces and said, "Did I interrupt anything?"

Jake and I both answered at once, "No, nothing. Nothing at all."

"Oh, that's good, because if I didn't know better, I would think there were some kind of problem. Glad to know I was wrong." He looked at us one more time and shook his head.

At that moment, everyone began piling in. In the next fifteen minutes, the group was assembled and seated.

"A good, good morning to you all." John was fresh and ready to go. "We should have a big fanfare of trumpets," he said, "because today's the day we finish the Random Function Identification of our very own . . .that is . . . Bob's inlet check valve."

Bob looked up. "All right, already!"

John grinned. "Okay. I give up."

"Once again, as we did with the mousetrap, we will apply two-word descriptions to each of the parts we didn't finish yesterday. You've had a night to sleep on it, but my guess is you didn't stay up all night thinking about it. Am I right?

"You bet!"

"Not me."

"I slept."

"Right. I thought a minute of inspiration might get the wheels turning again. You put on a good show for Dean yesterday with the valve. He told me he was impressed. So was I. As you finish this phase today, I know you're determined to do the best job you can to come up with the best solution as soon as you can."

"So if any of you still have any reluctance about expressing your ideas, please know that no one will criticize you for whatever you put on the table, laugh at you, or put you down for anything -- not even Jake."

"Huh?" said Jake.

"Now who'll manage the flip chart."

Bob raised his hand. "I'll do the chart if you promise not to give us any more of those quotations you have to uplift us. Where do you find those things, anyway?"

"I'll try, but I can't promise. It's an addiction."

"Gee, I'm sorry about that. I have one for you that's my favorite, though. Would you like to hear it?"

"I can take it. Go ahead."

"I forget who said it, but it goes like this: "Put a smile on your face in the morning, and get it over with."

"That's inspiring, Bob."

"I thought you'd like it."

When the laughter subsided, John said, "May we get on with this now?"

"Wait, John. If I work the chart, can I still put in my ideas? I have some doozies."

"Of course. I have my post-its, so let's go. Ready?"

"Yup."

"Great," said John. "Let's tackle the housing, now. Let 'em roll, folks."

I volunteered the first one, "Prevents corrosion."

Then came, "Supports weight."

"Reduces vibration."

"Distributes load."

The longer we worked, the more we immersed ourselves in the process. The Value Analysis job plan guided us much as an outline for a book, steering us toward a finite conclusion. It gave us the confidence to know where we were going, and what it was going to take to get us there . . . to a solution to our problem that would, in the end, affect our lives.

If that sounded dramatic, it's because it was. This was not destined to be just another new design to put on the market to make Alarum Aerospace, Inc. look attractive to investors. That made me feel so good, because I've always disliked and mistrusted companies that existed for that purpose alone.

This result would be what we'd heard over and over: 'the essence of Alarum Aerospace: a quality product built foremost to satisfy the customer's needs at a fair price.' I was thrilled to be here and be part of that, because all of us were an extension of that essence, taking a piece of it into our lives as a part of who we are. This place, where members of the group who had been here for years and spent the major part of their waking hours, had become a second home, and they were a family. I would want to do everything I could to protect that family, and present an image of quality and care for others, namely its customers.

There was no longer a question in anyone's mind that this workshop had to take precedence over everything else. The urgency was always on our minds, now, to the extent that we almost didn't want to take any breaks. But John reminded us that it was important to relax the intensity of the task and return refreshed and ready to go again.

When we looked up after we had described all the functions of the valve, post-it notes were everywhere. The walls were littered. We were closer to our goal, now, and we were ready for the next step.

"Time to take a breather," John called out. "Ten minutes," he said.

"Oh, no. Why not skip the coffee for once and get to the diagramming while we're hot," Doug said.

"Trust me, people," John said for the second time, "you'll do much better if you rest your brains a few minutes. We'll pick it up in ten. Calories at the back, as usual."

Can we do it? Will we be able to save Alarum Aerospace, or have we put in all this love and effort only to wind up in failure, anyway? How dramatic! What am I saying? It's only Tuesday. I've never been in this kind of a situation. All I do know is that all of us are giving it a hell of a try, and that has to count for something.

14

I wanted to check on the investigation board's findings of the flight incident again. The same office was available down the hall. I ran in and shut the door. But this time, I took off my watch and laid it on the desk in front of me. Pulling my cell phone out, I dialed the airline again. Not as a customer but as an engineer at Alarum Aerospace looking into the field failure.

"I'm sorry, Ms. Jamison, nothing is conclusive yet. I can tell you that they speculated that turbulence might be a factor. They also said the pilots received cockpit instrument warnings moments before the plane lost altitude. It was something about irregularity with the aircraft's elevator control, some glitch in the stabilization system and a faulty pitot static tube."

"Did they mention anything about an intake check valve?'

She paused a moment. "No, I didn't hear a word about that. Are you with the AOG team?"

I ignored the direct question about me being on the airplane-on-ground investigation team, "But they don't know anything for sure?"

"No. It's going to take some time. The NTSB has the flight data recorder and cockpit voice recorder, and they still have to interview the crew and passengers. I'm sorry, I hope this helps."

"I will have more research to do, but you've been very helpful. Thank you so much."

"You're welcome. Good luck with your project. Bye, now."

Ha! one minute to spare. I grabbed my watch, my phone and my notes and hightailed it out of there and back down the hall. I couldn't believe Jake was blocking the door. I bet he was waiting for me to come back late. He started to say something. I put up a cautioning finger and said, "Don't even think about it." For the first time, he shut his mouth and looked shocked. I went in, sat down and waited for John, anxious to get to work again.

We were back in our cozy circle. It began to feel like King Arthur (John) counseling us, the brave Alarum Aerospace Knights of the Roundtable (the team), gathered to save the company in its time of dire need. And so we were. On to FAST diagramming!

As soon as everyone was seated, he didn't waste any time. We all knew that Dean expected to see some results by the end of the week, and we did, too.

"All right, folks, before we get into the diagramming, I want to click on your 'refresh' key, in case yesterday was stale and forgotten."

Someone groaned. John stopped and looked around the table.

"I know. I realize this isn't easy. That's why I figure a little repetition can't hurt; it can only help. And you can check it against your notes and fill in where you might need it. Besides it may be on the test."

"So in summary, FAST diagramming, or the Function Analysis System Technique, is the evaluation process where you go through all those lovely post-its that came from your creative talents in the Random Function Identification phase. You will shorten that list by discussing the functions. The consensus you reach on each of those functions will be placed in connecting boxes in two-word descriptions answering 'HOW' and 'WHY'. If you'll look at your notes from yesterday, you'll see that the 'HOW' is on the left, and the 'WHY' is on the right and the critical path runs through the horizontal center of the chart. The discussions will stimulate you to think and create, and Bytheway will be pleased. That's how we will emerge with new ideas that have the best potential to consider for re-design purposes. Somebody wiser than I once said, 'You can tell if an idea is red-hot when somebody pours cold water on it, it retains its heat.'

Bob rolled his eyes. "Oh, boy! I guess it is an addiction."

"Bob, make yourself useful. Come up here and grab your marker. We even have a chart for you that's twice as big as the last one, with empty boxes, too."

"I have no words."

" The doozies you mentioned will do. Let us begin diagramming."

As each function was pulled from the Random Function Identification post-it pile, we discussed the function from every angle: basic function, efficiency, redundancy, weight, customer requirements and more. The discussions, themselves, were energizing and sometimes pretty intense. Even Leland joined in the melee. Not only did I find the give-and-take stimulating and informative, but also it brought me closer to my colleagues. I felt that I knew them better than I did before we began.

Sell functions, like aesthetic appeal, were also considered for selling points, but not placed on the critical path or major logic path, if used at all. Those functions gravitated to the "one time" or "all the time" function areas.

"Do we really need all of those sell functions?" asked Randy. That started another whole new debate.

One of the most important outcomes is that we were able to drop functions that were unnecessary, or did not fit with our objectives. There were so many of them, some of them even overlapped. It took time, but we were mindful of working as a team, and each decision was truly a consensus.

Even though we may have grown tired after a while because of the intensity, we still wanted to push forward to make it a success. Some of the team at first thought it was just an engineering exercise, but at the end of the day, we felt we had really accomplished something together. It was working. This Value Analysis process was working, and we all felt we had a real chance to save our company's reputation.

"Okay everyone, believe it or not, it's lunchtime." No one jumped up and ran. "Hey, you people not only need this, you deserve it. You're doing a great job. But you need fuel so you don't wind down."

"Same time, same place? asked Chip.

"Yeah, perfect," Bob agreed. "You coming, John? This time it's okay to talk about the valve."

"Great," said John.

15

It was sunshine and breezes again for our walk to the restaurant. People along the way were out manicuring their lawns and gardens, adding to the aroma of green things growing.

I looked around for Bob. I thought I might be able to talk with him about the plane decompressions and what I had learned so far. But he was walking ahead with John, deep in conversation. I didn't think it was my imagination, but he seemed a little cooler to me than he had been. In fact he didn't say two words to me all day, except a grumpy "hello." My eyes wandered to Jake, who looked to me to be unusually self-satisfied. I didn't want to connect the dots.

The two outdoor tables where we sat last time were available when we arrived at the restaurant, and the same pleasant waitress was there to serve us.

"Hi, Marie," I said. "We're back."

"Good," she said, "I hope you come back often."

None of us cared where we sat at the two tables. We grabbed whatever chair happened to be in front of us. Leland was my lunch mate this time.

"What do you think about Value Analysis," he asked, "Do you think it will do the job for us?"

"I think it's incredible. I'm so glad I was asked to be on this team. This may sound over-the-wall, but I almost feel as if I'm being let in on the secret of life."

He smiled. "Well, the life of the company, anyway. You may be right." he said.

Both of us were quiet for a moment, waiting for the waitress, who had almost made her way around the table to us. After she took our orders, I said, "Leland, do you mind if I ask you a question?" *He may be shy, but he's smart and has common sense.*

"Be careful. I'm old."

"That's funny, Leland." I gave him a shoulder nudge. "But it's not that kind of question. It's just that you were so nice about offering help. I hope you don't mind, but I need to trust you to keep this between us."

Leland's expression became serious. He said, "Of course, Michelle. Gossip isn't my thing. That wouldn't be helpful at all.

I hesitated. "Well, it's about Jake."

"Yes, I noticed he hasn't been too nice to you."

"He really resents me. I've tried to ignore it, but it's at the point where he's undermined my reputation with Bob, and he sabotaged me and it's only Tuesday. I think he sees me as a threat to his position. And, believe me, Leland, nothing could be farther from the truth."

The general table chat was toned down again; I had to lower my voice.

"What can I do? I don't want to make an enemy of Jake. I just want to become a good engineer."

"Hmmm, that is a problem. Let me think a moment . . . I'll tell you, Michelle, if it were me, I'd talk to both of them, and be honest about what's happened. It's got to be hard to focus when that sort of thing goes on. Let them work it out with you. Then you won't have the whole responsibility on your shoulders."

I told Leland what my dad suggested.

"That's great! Even better," he said. Why can't you do both? After you've talked it out with Bob, go to Jake with that idea. He might be more receptive to it then. He might love it." He started to laugh. "Heck, you might have a friend for life."

"Leland, you're wonderful! If we weren't in a restaurant, I'd kiss your cheek."

That prompted a little pink to creep up his face. "Oh, I didn't do anything, but I'm still here for you. I'd like to see you succeed."

"Thank you so much."

At that psychological moment, John called for the crew to return. I think Leland was relieved.

16

We came back to the meeting room, settled down, and looked to John to see where he would take us next. We didn't have to wait long. He was as anxious as we were to get into it again.

Bob spoke up. "John, I have to admit, I was too quick to judge VA when we first began. I didn't realize how it would put us back on track. I can't believe what we've accomplished so far. We already have ideas and we haven't even started brainstorming ideas. Thanks for getting us there."

We all nodded and expressed our agreement:

"Right! It felt great.."

"Yeah! Look at what we've done."

"I didn't think it was possible."

"I thought it would be a big waste of time. I guess I was wrong.

"We're with you, John. What have you got for us next? Let's go," said Bob.

"And I'm with you," John said. "You people are easy to teach, because you're bright and talented. But there is more. Do you remember the Pareto Chart, way back at the beginning? You can consult your notes. This will be the last step in the function phase. What we will do now is take all the functions we haven't eliminated and apply a cost to each one using a cost function worksheet. I have to warn you, this will take a while to assess and won't be easy, but when it's over, you'll be astonished at the results -- just as we were when we ferreted out the valve we came to use."

And so we began. First we did a study to determine total costs per unit. Then, part by part, we attached cost to each of the functions. *John was right. This is tedious. Where is it taking us? We were just starting to get some good ideas and now we're arguing about how much cost should be allocated to the function 'attach components'? Hey, wait a minute...*

"Look at all those costs for function 'attach components'!" I blurted out. My hand went over my mouth. "Sorry, but that's unbelievable."

"You see, I knew you'd make discoveries like that," John said. "You can also see redundancy by all the parts that have the function 'attach components'."

It took us the rest of the afternoon to emerge with three of the most expensive and most redundant functions we identified as the best candidates for change. We transferred the costs to the FAST diagram for a vivid visual representation of how are costs were distributed across functions.

At times, I wondered how many of us would be friends when this was over. Since everything we decided was on a consensus basis, there were moments I thought that if we were in court, we would be a hung jury. But we did work hard and well together, with the same goal -- to create a product with parameters that everyone at first said would be impossible. I looked into the eyes of my colleagues, and I saw that we were a team.

John checked his watch. "Okay, guys, Quitting time. Good job. If you take a look at the FAST diagram what do you see?" We all gathered around the visual functional representation of our project and studied it in silence.

Bob was the first one to speak up, "Most of our cost are in the secondary functions."

"Exactly!" replied John. "The basic function – what the part needs to do – is a fraction of the total cost. The secondary functions are the means by which you chose to support the basic function. It is your design approach. On that note, let's regroup bright and early tomorrow."

"Let's stay a little longer and continue." Doug suggested. "We've come so far.

"Na-ah, we've got brainstorming to do tomorrow, and you can't do that with the fuzzy heads you must have by now. Besides, the college wants us out of here by 5:30. So have a good night. See you tomorrow."

17

As I left the building I couldn't help but look back on the day. Sure, I was happy that things were going well at the office with the actual work. Relationships? Not so much. Tension increased between Jake and me. I couldn't ignore it much longer if I wanted to save my career or my sanity. I worked hard and studied hard. Aside from the workshop, I tried to be creative and develop and offer new ideas. Even though I'd been there just a couple days it felt like months. Bob's coolness accelerated; he barely listened or spoke to me anymore.

I reached the car and pressed the remote. I was glad I was able to drive it here this time. A walk back to the office was not on my favorite list today. My hand was on the door handle when I noticed a piece of paper under my windshield wiper. At first I thought it was a ticket. No reason for it that I could think of. I took a closer look. It was a note. I reached over and pulled it off the window. My hand shook as I opened the fold. I had to lay it up against the car to keep it steady so I could read it. It was from Sally, as I feared. The note said, "Did you think I forgot you the way you ignored me? I'll always remember what you did. You need to be punished, so you will never forget again. Wait for it!"

"Oh, my God!" I breathed. That feeling in the pit of my stomach, it was there again. But this time, it wasn't butterflies. More like bees. I turned around in a complete circle. My eyes searched the parking lot and every tree and bush. I only saw people going to and from their cars. I yanked open my front door. I checked the back seat before I

leaped in behind the wheel and started the car. When all the
doors locked automatically at ignition, I closed my eyes and
said a little prayer of thanks, blessing the manufacturer. I flew
out of the lot as fast as I could, hoping my heart would stay
in my chest. That trip home was one of the longest short
drives I had ever taken.

Before I could put the key in the front door, my
mother opened it, smiling, and said, "Hi, Princess. You look
terrible."

"Thanks, Mom. I love you, too."

"Hard day?"

"You could say that."

"Well, there's a nice dinner waiting for you. Sit down
and eat. You'll feel better."

That was so "Mom." It was her panacea for
everything. The funny thing was it worked most of the time.
And her kiss "hello" had already helped.

"Hi, Dad."

"Hi, Princess. Ready for dinner? I'm starved and
mom wouldn't let me start until you got here."

"Ready if you are."

Mom whispered, "He's cruised the kitchen, sniffing
the pots for the last half-hour. I had to pull him away from
them twice."

We sat down at Mom's usual perfect table to eat her
usual perfect dinner. The smells alone were wonderful. She
served spinach lasagna in a marinara sauce, a huge Caesar
salad, garlic bread, Birch Creek Cellars St. Jillian's Reserve
and home made tiramisu. The wine and good food worked
their wonders, and I began to calm down. Of course, none of
us could move afterwards. We were as stuffed as the lasagna.

"Okay, now give," Mom said. "What's going on?"
She refilled our wine glasses.

"It's that young man again, isn't it?" Dad said.

"Bill, let her talk!"

"She is talking." Poor Dad got a "tsk" and a dirty look.

What should I tell them about first? I can't keep Sally a secret much longer. It's become serious. She even knows where I live. She called my parents for my cell number, for heaven's sake. I'd better take one thing at a time, though. It's too much to lay on them at once. Can I just enjoy desert?

"Yes, Dad, it's Jake. He's gotten worse. I really think he'd like to see me out of there. In a way, I feel sorry for him. He's so obsessed with this, I don't know how he can think straight."

"Never mind that. What's he doing now?"

"For one thing, he worked on my boss again. I overheard him just this morning saying, 'I want to give Michelle the benefit of the doubt, but I've watched her make a lot of mistakes.' I don't even know what he means, Dad. We've been in the workshop the whole time."

"Did you confront him about it?"

"Yes, in the hall outside our meeting room, and he said, 'You misheard me. I defended you. He wanted to know where certain papers are that I had you fill out at his request. Remember? He doesn't appreciate your lack of professionalism. Maybe this company isn't the place for you'. Then he walked away."

"I don't know what else he's told him, but my boss barely talks to me now. Then Jake conveniently forgot to tell me about a conference call I was supposed to attend before this morning's workshop. That could impact my professional standing, too."

"But that's awful," Mom said. "You've got to do something, Michelle. You can't let this go on."

"I know, but I want to hold off until this project is over. I think, though, when I do make a move, it won't be planned. It'll be, 'Okay, now is the time. I've had enough'. That's when I'll speak my piece."

"But, princess, is that safe?" Dad asked. "How long will that take? Do you think it's wise to wait?"

"I'll try, Dad. It shouldn't be more than a couple of days."

"I hope not. That stress can ruin more than your career. It can ruin your health."

"I know. I expected some initial resentment, but nothing like this. It should be over soon."

"Well, get some rest tonight. You'll be fresh in the morning."

Mom wouldn't let me help her with the dishes, so I finished my wine while I watched a little television. By the time I hit the hay, I felt less brave about holding out for those couple of days than I did at dinner. I guessed I would see tomorrow.

I was so tired. It felt good to climb into bed. My face found the pillow. I was sure I would be asleep in two seconds. Instead I heard an eerie voice in my ear.

"Hello fellow traveler. Aren't you in bed a little early tonight?"

18

I opened my eyes and gasped. "Oh, my God! Sally! What are you doing here? How did you get in here?"

"You sleep with your window open, don't you? I'm pretty spry for my age. You have no idea what I can do -- and will do."

"Get out of here before I call the police."

"Never mind me. Your parents will never find you. They would want to take care of you, but now they can't. You don't deserve it, because you didn't take care of me."

Something in her hand caught the reflection of a small patch of light that shone in the room -- something that was buried halfway up her sleeve. I couldn't tell what it was at first, until the point of the blade was exposed.

"No! No-o-o-oh! Don't touch me!"

I tossed my blanket over her head and flew out of bed. It confused her long enough for me to get through the window -- the same window Sally had come through to enter the house. I landed in a flowerbed where the earth had just been turned over into soft mounds. It cushioned my fall, and I sprang up on my bare feet as fast as I could. I started to run.

I looked around me in panic. I didn't recognize anything I saw. The outside of my parents' house didn't look the same. I heard a noise behind me, but I couldn't tell how close it was. I was sure it was Sally. It was so dark! It had to be her. And that knife! I knew it was meant for me. I ran even faster. My heart raced. My breath came heavier. I felt the stones in the path I ran on dig into the bottoms of my feet, and I cried out in pain. Perspiration coated my face and body and soaked into my nightgown. The footsteps sounded closer. The clatter of the stones grew louder. I was exhausted and grew weaker. The sweat made me slip. I almost fell. I didn't think I could run much farther. I could sense her right behind me, nearly touching me. I screamed as loud as I could, but there was no one there to hear.

The lights went on in my room. Both my parents grabbed me at the same time.

"Michelle! What happened! Are you all right? Sh-sh-sh! It's okay. We're here now."

"You were having a nightmare."

I sat up, crying, trying to shake myself awake and back to reality.

"Bill, she's all perspired! I'm going to get a cold cloth."

"Calm down. Now, princess, are you okay?" My dad's face was strained with concern.

Mom was back in a flash to mop my face and neck. That did help, and I began to come back to normal. Dad handed me my robe and slippers.

"Let's get you a cup of tea, and you can tell us what upset you so," Mom said. "You haven't screamed like that since your brother cut your bangs in 5th grade."

Mom poured the steamed, fragrant tea and sweetened it with honey for good measure. The hot liquid felt good on its way down. My parents drank their tea and waited. After I took a couple of sips, I looked at them and said, "I'm being stalked."

"What!" They both exclaimed at the same time. Mom's mouth dropped open; Dad choked on his tea and had a coughing spell.

"Is it that boy again? I'll kill him," he said between coughs.

"No, Dad. He's just scared for his career. I wasn't going to tell you about my stalker right away, because I didn't want to upset you, and I didn't think it was serious at first. I thought she would fade away."

"She -- a woman?" asked Mom.

"Yes. She's an older woman, 65, I'd say. I met her on the plane coming in and changed seats with her so she could be near the window. She was afraid to fly." I told them the story, including the first e-mail. "And now I see her or signs of her everywhere. She said you guys even gave her my cell phone number. She was the 'friend from college', remember?"

"Oh, for heaven's sake!" Mom said, "I'm so sorry. I'll never give out your number again."

"How could you know? But now I think she has become dangerous."

"What about a protection order?"

"How would that help, Dad? Besides, I don't even know her last name or where she lives."

"Well, I'll contact the police today and see what we can do. In the meantime, Michelle, I don't want you to take chances. Don't go out at night, especially alone, don't work late, and do not walk or travel in isolated places."

"No worries, Dad. I'll be careful."

"You'd better go back to bed and try to get some sleep. You won't be able to get up for work in the morning."

"I'll be okay. Thank you both" I kissed them goodnight. "I'll tell you one thing, though. I will sleep with my window closed and locked the rest of tonight."

19

I didn't forget that our latest instructions were to go straight to the community college meeting room every morning until the workshop was over. I made it on time, but Jake was already there with a smug expression on his face. I had a feeling he made an extra effort to get there before me.

"Good morning," I said. "Hope you have a nice day today."

"Uh, thanks," he said grudgingly.

Okay, that was it. This was ridiculous. I need to talk to Bob today. It was impossible to work in this climate. I didn't think it could happen, but it was harder to keep my mind on whatever was at hand. At least one thing had to be settled right away – either Sally or Jake.

John strode into the room as fresh and awake as ever. How does he do it? He took one look at us and said, "The same two sourpusses as yesterday morning. It's depressing. You know, that could ruin a person's day. Why don't you both go to a gym and fight it out?"

Neither of us thought that was funny. No time for a response, though, because the whole clan piled in at once, ready to hit the day running. The workshop would be more exciting now as we entered the creativity phase. We had a real chance at success, and the Jake-and-I thing didn't seem to matter at this moment.

"Good mo-o-o-o-rning BMW!"

"Good morning, John," everyone said in unison, like a second grade class.

John started to laugh. "Thank you. That was nice. Are you ready to go?"

A room full of applause was the answer.

"As a reminder," he said, "you remember what the Pareto chart of the Cost Function Worksheet showed you yesterday, right? It left you with the three most expensive functions. Today, we will brainstorm those functions and see what we come up with for ideas. We won't argue or discuss as we wade through what is called the Speculation or Creative Phase, because you're about to open your minds to all possibilities."

"Forget all the rules," John said. "Be brave and creative and think outside the box, and don't stop to evaluate anything. Just let the ideas flow, no matter where they come from. James Bryant Conant, who was a chemist, educator and President of Harvard University from 1933 to 1953 said, 'Behold the turtle -- he made progress only when he stuck his neck out.'"

"I'll be darned," said Bob. "He did it again – another corny quote. There's probably a 12 step program to help you with that addiction."

"You will look at these functions as you had never thought to look at them before," continued John. "Can these functions be achieved in different ways? Over the years, many new materials have been developed. Can any of these -- lighter, stronger, more durable, less expensive, more available -- replace the older products? Think in terms of 'What if . . . ' Could this or that be done in a different way, easier, or with more efficiency? Never stop questioning. Let your minds expand. Reach for things you never dreamed of before. Open up those tight little corners of your minds and let the fresh air flow in, and in this phase, eliminate nothing. Let's go!"

"Okay, coach!" Bob called.

And, boy! Did we go! We brainstormed each of the three top functions, and emerged with over one hundred ideas per function.

"Wow!" was the general reaction. We never expected to come up with that many.

As before, we hoped that John would just let us continue on, but he insisted on a break. "Ten minutes and a cup of high-octane coffee can only help," he said, "not to mention the sugar high from the pastry."

20

This was my moment, and I seized it. I caught Bob as he was on his way to the coffee urn. I could feel Jake's eyes bore right through my back, but I ignored him.

"Good morning, Bob. May I talk with you for a moment, alone?"

"Hi, Michelle. Yes, we can talk, but can it wait? "

It was obvious he was not thrilled. "How about during lunch? I'd appreciate it. I need your help. I've been up all night over this, and to be frank, I feel it could mean the end of my career."

His eyes narrowed a little. I could tell he was trying to measure my words.

"All right, Michelle. It's a date. We'll do lunch."

"Thanks, Bob."

I went out to the ladies' room to freshen up, and to utter a quiet prayer that what I was about to say to Bob wouldn't be the end of life for me at Alarum Aerospace.

When we finished our break, we were only too happy to get back to the work we didn't want to be interrupted in the first place. But John was right. If there were anybody sagging, it was no longer apparent.

"Now that you're recharged," John said. "I know you'll do well with the next phase, Evaluation. Each one of the ideas that challenged your imagination in the Creative Phase will now become the object of team discussion again, but with a little more structure. The question: Will the idea improve the performance of any of the three functions chosen for your project, or should it be eliminated?"

"What, exactly, are we looking for, John, so we don't waste time?"

"I'm sure you people know that better than I do. First, in order to get to the best ideas, you need to get rid of the ones you're sure won't work. Then you need to talk about the major pros and cons of each idea that remains, including the cost, time, and how it will affect performance, until you boil them down to the best ones that you all agree can be developed further. And, team BMW, on these you must agree."

We jumped right in where we left off, placed all the ideas that remained in categories, and found the least recurring costs. Then we combined the lowest cost ideas to create proposals for our project. We felt like we were getting somewhere. It seems there's a little artist in all of us, because we sketched those ideas on flip charts, discussed them and labeled them alphabetically. Bonus, each new idea improved as it was sketched and discussed, inspired by the one before it, and we were able to narrow down the list to a much smaller number we felt was viable for the Development Phase.

When I looked up, John was trying to get our attention.

I heard him say, "Okay, everybody, time for a breather."

No one else seemed to notice. We were so into what we were doing, he was just part of the background noise.

"Hey, gang! Listen up, please."

I guess we were still too much involved, so he put two fingers in his mouth and gave that whistle that makes your hat fly off. *Even with four brothers, I've never been able to do that.*

"Wow!" John said. "I think I need to requisition a megaphone."

All heads turned to watch Leland and Chip still going at it. The two of them stopped at the sudden silence, a little embarrassed.

"Thank you, gentlemen," said John. "Now, I know the clock hasn't seemed to move for you, folks, but I'm afraid it is time for lunch. Believe me, this will wait for you until you get back."

No one argued, as we got ready to shuffle out.

"Same restaurant?" Chip asked the team, heading for the door.

"Sure," said Doug from the end of the line. He turned and called back, "Well, are you coming, John?"

"You bet." He hurried after us.

I was nervous. It wasn't just the discussion with Bob, although that would have been enough by itself. But Sally -- I was afraid she might show up again.

21

Jake made it his business to walk with Bob to the restaurant. I guess I expected that he would. That guy not only upset me at every opportunity, but he made himself miserable as well. I hoped I was about to change that.

When we arrived, the place seemed a little more crowded than usual. Bob excused himself from Jake, and managed to find us a table not far from the group, but enough removed so that we might talk.

The waitress came by to take our orders. She wasn't a minute too soon. I was hungry, and everything smelled so good. Besides, it's better not to have a serious discussion on an empty stomach. I don't know who said that. I guess I did.

While Bob ordered his lunch, I glanced at Jake. Of course, there was a frown on his face. That was a shame. He was a handsome guy. He'd be much better looking if he smiled now and then, instead of being so grumpy.

"Okay, Michelle," Bob said, "tell me what it is that has kept you up at night?"

"Not 'what', Bob. It's 'who'."

"Jake, right?"

"I'm afraid so. And I think I understand why, at least in his mind. He's running scared. For some reason he's got it in his head that I'm out to get his job, or at least show him up somehow. That doesn't even make sense. I'm right out of college, and he has years of experience. He's been here for two years, for heaven's sake. And I would never do that to him, anyway."

"Bob, I don't know what terrible things he's told you about me. But you need to know that he's trying to sabotage me. He would like me out of here."

"How would you know that?"

"For starters, I overheard him tell you, 'I'd like to give her the benefit of the doubt, but I've watched her make a lot of mistakes'." Bob, that's not even possible. We've been at the workshop most of the time. And when I confronted him, he said I misunderstood, that he was defending me. And remember that important phone call I missed? Did you ask him to tell me to be there?"

"Yes, I did."

"He never told me. I would have been on the call. He also told me to shut up at meetings and let you and him do all the talking, so I wouldn't embarrass the department. Bob, he's been rude and nasty to me since day one at every opportunity, and I don't think I can take it anymore."

"I'm sorry to hear all this. I wasn't aware how serious it was. What would you like me to do? Do you want me to talk to him?"

"No, thank you, that would only make matters worse. But I do have a couple of suggestions, if you don't mind."

"Okay, what are they?"

"First, when you schedule meetings, can you please notify me by my e-mail?"

"No problem."

"Thank you. Also, what do you think about my presence at your meetings with Jake for a while? Maybe that would improve our work relationship, and he won't give you the wrong impression of me anymore."

"I'm not sure about that one. I'll think about it, though. What else?"

"How about if I leave a weekly report on your desk? Or it could even be a running log. It could summarize my activities and accomplishments. Then nothing could be disputed."

"Hmmm . . . let me think about that, too, Michelle. I'll let you know. I must say your suggestions are constructive."

"I know that complaining doesn't solve anything, Bob. And if this goes on, it will hurt our work and the company. Besides, I know Jake's been good for you and the department for the two years he's been here. I wouldn't want to do anything to disturb that. And, in spite of it all, I like Jake. I think it's because I understand him. He's as unhappy about this as he's making me. And in that case, neither one of us can give you our best."

"Oh, and one last thing I thought about that might do the most good. Maybe we can find a project where he can be my mentor. Is that possible? That way, he'll have more recognition, he'll stop worrying about me and his job, and his ego will be intact."

"You really are a sweet girl, Michelle. I'm glad you came to me with this. We'll see what we can do. Meanwhile, eat your lunch before it gets cold."

22

Back from lunch, fueled up, and ready to go! John was seated and thoughtful. We took another look at the ideas that were sketched and considered for possible proposal, and evaluated the negatives and positives -- that is, until we were about half way through the alphabet.

"Well, people," Bob said, "it looks like there are no further suggestions. Now what, John?"

Our consultant had watched our progress, our enthusiasm and our desire to meet the challenge over the past few days. I sensed that he felt a connection to us, as if he were responsible for either our ultimate success or failure. He stood up and gazed around the table at our motley crew. Ties were loosened, collar buttons hung open, and some looked as though they had run their fingers through their hair several times. Chewing gum and hard candy wrappers decorated the table, along with the wet rings and plastic bottles from the water consumed.

John looked at the mess and said, "If it were within my power to reward this group, you would have it. You worked hard to answer a call for your company at a time of crisis, and nobody could have done a better job."

We glanced at each other through tired eyes, smiled, and leaned back in our chairs to catch our breath. We felt pretty proud of ourselves, but knew we had more work ahead and a deadline to meet.

"And now, John?" asked Randy.

"And now," said John, "this is Development Phase time, where you filter down the proposals you have, and vote on mutually exclusive ones. You're about to pin down your value alternatives, and you will have to document those proposals with written descriptions, justifications to support them, sketches, performance assessments, calculations and cost comparisons."

"Wow!" said Randy. "That's a lot of paper."

"Yes, and a lot of work, but all of you won't be required to do all of it -- not if you're organized and have a plan."

"What do you mean?"

"I mean teamwork. You all have talent and specialties. Use them. To obtain some of the information you will need to create value alternatives, you will work as a whole team, of course. But a large portion of the work can be assigned to single members who might have easier access to or expertise in certain aspects. When you've gathered all the knowledge necessary concerning the best proposals you intend to consider, cast a collective eagle eye to be sure you have left no unanswered questions.

"Okay? Do you have any questions for me?"

The room was quiet, pregnant with everyone's thoughts about the activities of the past few days and with what we'd just heard. Leland was the only one with any movement. He was doodling on the paper in front of him. I saw him stop and look at what he had penciled there.

"No, John, we'll just get to it," said Bob. "Let's vote."

As we roused ourselves to begin the multi-vote to narrow down our proposals to the final three, Leland spoke, breaking the silence.

"You know," he said, "what would happen if we took the basic function design that we have and combine that with one of these new ideas?"

It took a second for what he said to sink in. Then it was like a fresh breeze had blown into the room and re-energized everyone. His proposal went up on the flip chart, even the sketch I had thought was a doodle, and the clamor began again. When the discussion was finished and the consensus reached, I shouted "Oh my God, I think he did it! Leland did it!"

Indeed he did. The end result used the existing reed valve technology. It added a second reed valve for additional functionality. That decreased flow restriction. Then it embedded the reed valves in an air supply line, which eliminated the need for the expensive housing and associated support structure attachments, and that reduced its mass. It was remarkable, but when all was said and done, the total cost was reduced by 70%.

We thought we would be able to find a satisfactory solution, but we never imagined it would be anything like this, and so soon. Nobody did.

"Incredible! And you guys thought you weren't creative!" John said with a big smile. Dean will never believe this. And just in time for your break. As a reward, you can even have a second cup of coffee."

None of us could contain our excitement. We grabbed each other and jumped up and down like a major league baseball team that had just won the World Series. Jake was holding my hand, and his other arm was around my shoulder. When he realized it, his eyes opened wide, and he stopped short and backed away. I didn't know what to do, so I smiled.

John happened to look our way at just that moment. "That's more like it," he said.

After fifteen minutes of back patting and congratulating each other, especially Leland, over coffee and donuts, John brought us back to reality, and we all settled down.

"The workshop is in session again," he said. "Value alternatives are waiting for us. That means we're on the home stretch. Once we have reviewed the alternatives and documented the results of our research and rationale for those we've accepted, we can begin the Presentation Phase.

But I'm getting ahead of myself. I don't want to confuse you."

Everyone was quiet, with rapt attention focused on John. He stopped to take a breath.

That's when my phone rang. I felt about two feet tall. I had forgotten to turn it off. I remembered, though, that I needed the voice mail, so it couldn't be turned off at that point, either. I blushed several shades of pink, excused myself and left the room. I had to stay out until I was sure the voice mail had come through, and the voice mail notice hit the screen. It was from a public phone. I knew it was Sally. I didn't listen to it, of course.

When I returned, John said, "Is everything all right? You look pale."

"Yes. I'm sorry."

"Okay. We're good. Doug, can you man the chart, please?"

"Sure.

We were already excited about the system we had redesigned. Now we debated and discussed until we reached the consensus necessary to develop a short list from the remaining proposals. Then we organized the assignments and work we would have to do to clearly define the value alternatives for each of the three ideas selected for further development. All things considered, it wasn't a bad day at the office.

John's voice filtered through the chatter. "Attention, folks. It's that time of day. I bet you didn't even realize it. But you can go home, now, and dream about today's success. Have a great night."

23

With the excitement over what John and our team had accomplished, I was at my highest high. A few of the group were going out for a small celebration, but I excused myself and managed to break away from the crowd and head toward my car. It had been a long day, and I knew Mom had prepared something special for dinner. She always does. I didn't want to disappoint her. And, oh yes, Dad had cautioned me not to go home alone after dark.

My highest high was replaced by my lowest low as that old sick feeling reminded me that I had to watch out for Sally. That sensation, I thought as I made my way to the lot, could almost be compared to the decompression I experienced on the plane when we dropped thousands of feet in seconds. I didn't know what that woman was capable of yet, but when I found the note under my windshield wiper, I understood that other people in the lot, going to and from their cars, were not something that would stop her. It made me wonder whether the nightmare I had that starred Sally foreshadowed what she would do -- or was it my own fear in high gear?

My chariot awaited me an aisle away – *I really need to get a non-mom car. But it did provide the basic function of 'transport me' I guess I could wait awhile to add that expensive secondary function 'impress friends'.* I stepped up my pace, turning my head in every direction. When I reached the car, I was about to press the remote, but it fell out of my hand. I bent down and grabbed it up as fast as I could. I was so nervous, I dropped it again. "Oh, no!" I looked wildly around before I scooped it up and unlocked the door. I made sure the back seat was empty before I slipped in behind the wheel, slammed the door and locked it. I didn't wait for the ignition to lock it for me this time. Then it occurred to me I was holding my breath. That's when I started to breathe again.

On the twenty-minute drive home, I turned on some music and tried to relax. I didn't want my parents to see me on edge. It was difficult to keep things from them; they always seem to know when something's wrong. I thought about Jake. I was confused. What happened there? He seemed shocked when he discovered his arm on my shoulder and my hand in his. Was that an accident or an epiphany? And all I could do was smile back? What was that? Why am I even thinking about that? I'm sure we'll be back to normal tomorrow, whatever normal is.

As I neared the folk's driveway, I thought it might be safer to honk the horn a couple of times, since Sally hadn't shown up yet. It was too quiet out there. On the second honk, the curtains were drawn back at the window, and within seconds, Mom and Dad appeared at the door. They'll never know what a welcome sight they were.

I gathered some things out of the car from work that I wanted to study, my purse, and a cardigan sweater in case it became chilly in the air-conditioning. *In Chicago more people wear sweaters during the summer than in the winter.* I watched the area around me as I locked the car door, glad that my parents were standing there. I almost ran into their arms.

"Hello, Mom. Hi, Dad. Did you have a nice day?"

"Very pleasant. Not much excitement. Sometimes we like it that way," Mom said. "And you?"

"Well, I can't say the same," I said as we moved on into the house. I'm worn out from the excitement. We reached our goal on the project we've been working on, and then some. It was a thrill. Nobody thought we could, but we even surpassed it!"

"Good for you! That's wonderful." That came from both of them.

"Oh, Mom! Those heavenly aromas again. What are they? No! Don't tell me. Let me be surprised."

"It's really not a big deal this time, Princess. I didn't feel much like cooking today, so I just threw a small brisket into the oven. And, you know, that practically cooks itself. So do the baked potatoes. The sautéed veggies needed a little watching, but not much."

"Does your 'not a big deal' include baked Alaska for dessert?"

"No, not exactly." She laughed. "How's a peach cobbler with vanilla ice cream?"

"I'll forgive you. Mom, you're unbelievable. Maybe you should have sent me to cooking school instead of Embry-Riddle."

"Seriously, Michelle, that was an easy dinner, and I could never do what you do. That's where you shine."

I had to give her a big kiss for that one -- and then gorge myself on her "easy" dinner.

When we were through eating, I asked, "Say, how are the boys? I haven't seen them since I've been home."

"Well," said Dad, "Because their jobs took one to England and the other three all over the United States, it's been a little difficult for them, except to call you when you got home. But they'll all be here in a couple of weeks. That's the earliest they could make it.

"Wow, that's great! What's the occasion?"

They both just looked at me.

"Mom? Dad?"

"It's you, Michelle."

24

"Oh, no! You didn't tell them about Sally!"

"Michelle, they would want to know. They would be so upset if we didn't tell them."

"Mom, I'm a grown woman. I can handle this."

"You can't handle a mental case by yourself. Besides, you'll always be their baby sister."

"Speaking of Sally," Dad said, "I went to the police today, and had a talk with a detective."

"You did? What did he say? What can I do? Will they go after her?"

"He admits she's scary, but they can't do anything yet, because you've only had three actual encounters with her, and they haven't been violent."

"Dad, you mean if they're just threats, they won't do anything?"

"They will, if it continues, but first we have to have a safety plan. Let's go in the den, and I'll get my notes. You coming, Mary?"

"I'll be right there, as soon as I put the food away."

We managed to get off our chairs after stuffing ourselves at dinner. That canceled the bikini I had planned to buy for the pool. We arranged ourselves on the couch, and Dad laid everything out on the table in front of it.

"Mary?"

"I'm coming!"

Mom squeezed in next to me, so she could see Dad's notes, too.

"I'm glad I cautioned you about safety when you told us about this, Michelle. Guess what the police said about that?" Dad ranted on while I drifted back to the workshop. *If we uncovered that much potential in just one assembly, how much more are we missing at the system level? How much more can we increase value for the customer?*

"You're kidding!" Mom said.

"Well, it makes sense, doesn't it?" Dad looked at me. "See, I wasn't being over-protective, like you always think we are."

"I know, Dad."

"Give us the rest of it, Bill."

"I am. They told me Sally is what's classified as a Resentful Stalker. They are motivated by revenge and often try to intimidate by frightening their victims. The good news is they are the least likely to physically harm their victims. They said it's critical that you maintain a log of the incidents and her behavior from the beginning, for a couple of reasons. In case you have to testify later, you won't be fuzzy about what happened, or how often, and in case you want to apply for a restraining order."

"Mmm, I'm still not sure about the restraining order part, Dad. How would we even find her without her last name and address?" *So putting that into what I've been learning this week Sally's basic function is to 'intimidate victim'. What's the higher order function of that? 'Satisfy Ego'?*

"Michelle are you listening to your father?" scolded mom.

"Here's the interesting thing. The detective told me they could get that information from the airline. They have her seat number for that flight and everything. They wouldn't give it to us, but they will give it to the police under certain circumstances."

"That would be great! It means there's a chance that we might find her after all. But then what? She's a regular Houdini about disappearing."

"The police have their ways. They also said that even if she ignored an order, the fact that it was issued would be considered additional evidence. By the way, Michelle, on the

log, be sure to include any stalking-related behavior of any
kind, like . . .wait a minute. Let me see what I wrote here . . .
'harassing phone calls, letters, e-mail messages, acts of
vandalism, and threats communicated through third parties.'
Do you still have that e-mail you told us about that she sent
you?"

"I don't know. I'll have to take a look when I get to
work."

"If you have it, print it out and attach it to the form
after you log it in. If not, just log it."

"Okay. Anything else?"

"Let's see . . .yes. When you report the incident to
the police, the detective told me, always write down the
officer's name and badge number on the log sheet. Even if
the officers don't make an arrest, you can ask them to make a
written report and request a copy for your records. And here,
Princess, I picked up a couple of log forms for you. I hope to
God you won't need more than one."

"Thanks, Dad, and you, too, Mom for all the
support."

"You want to talk support, wait until your brothers
get into town."

"Oh, my God! I forgot about that. They'll want to
help the police."

"Maybe that wouldn't be a bad idea."

"Dad, really!"

"Bill, what about the phone." Mom asked. "Did the
detective tell you what to do about that? Shouldn't she
change the number or something?"

"As a matter of fact, he did. I was getting to that,
and the computer, too." Dad grabbed his notes again. "For
one thing, the detective advised that you do not use your
phone anymore."

"But, Dad. What am I supposed to do? I have to
have a phone."

"We'll get another one and keep it unlisted. She
knows the one you have, and she might have a GPS enabled

phone to track yours where ever you go. Don't throw that one away, though. Attach it to voice mail. Have the second one close by at all times, and put 911 and our numbers on speed dial. That's what the police suggested."

"This is horrible, Bill." said Mom, "She's really under siege."

"I know. It occurred to me that we should unlist a new number for our home phone. After all, she called us, too."

"What about my computer? She e-mailed me on the one at work."

"Michelle, just don't use it for anything personal. And above all, the policeman said not to respond to her in any way. Not by phone, computer, or if she shows up. The reason is stalkers want the contact, even if it's negative. It reinforces their behavior. But if she sends you any more e-mails, be sure to print them out and save them."

Stalkers want attention? So is my basic function correct? Or is the basic function 'receive attention'? I better pay attention before mom calls me out again...

"One last thing. You'd better tell people at work, stores, or anyone you've done business with since you've been home, not to give out any information at all about you. And make sure you change passwords on any accounts you have, like the bank."

Dad was quiet for a minute. So was Mom. It was obvious how disturbed they were by all this, though not more than I was. They probably felt as though they were failing at their basic parental function: 'protect child'.

"You know, Princess," Dad said, "if she acts out one more time, I think we'll contact the police. I don't want to wait and take any chances. In some cases, the detective told me, they'll even send out a police car for surveillance. Another option is the Civil Restraining Order I mentioned. But I guess there are different levels of this thing, and we'll have to see what happens. Let's hope it doesn't get any worse."

25

I stayed up late and watched television for a while, because I knew sleep was still out of the question. There was too much on my mind. It was hard to believe that because I felt sorry for someone on a plane, my whole life turned upside down. Is there a lesson there somewhere? I hope not. I'd hate to be the kind of person who didn't care. Isn't one of life's basic functions 'help others'?

At last I fell into bed long after Mom and Dad had retired. Best to try to put all that out of my mind and get some sleep. It should be a great day at work tomorrow, preparing the presentation for managerial approval of all our hard work. If I'm lucky, maybe Jake will be halfway decent, too. Those are things to look forward to. I try to be positive. That isn't always easy.

At last I started to doze. My phone rang a few times before I was conscious enough to pick it up. My parents came running in and Dad yelled, "Wait! Let it go to voice mail. Don't pick it up!"

"What are you two doing up? It's midnight."

"Couldn't sleep," said Mom. It's Sally, isn't it?"

"Who else would it be at this hour?"

"I don't really want to hear what this sick mind has to say. But let's listen to it. Maybe it will give us a clue about how to find her."

We played back Sally's raspy voice. "Hello, Michelle, I've missed you. I haven't spoken to you for a couple of days. I've been busy planning your punishment, you see." She laughed. "I bet you'd like to know what that is, wouldn't you? I enjoyed doing that. I love teaching a lesson to someone as thoughtless as you! I know you'll love it, too. Wait for it." She laughed a crazy laugh again, and hung up.

My mother began to cry. Dad said, "That's it! I'm calling the police right now," and he left the room. Mom wiped her eyes, put her arms around me and gave me a kiss.

"You'll be fine, Princess. We'll see to that. But don't forget, you'll have to take precautions, too."

She followed Dad from the room to hear what the police had to say. He was able to talk to the same detective with whom he'd spoken before, it turned out. The good news was the police would initiate an official case and begin looking for her right away, starting with the airline.

"He also suggested," Dad said, "that if she shows up in person, you use your phone and try to take a picture of her. That would be a big help. See if you can get some sleep, Princess. We'll see you later."

"Thanks, Dad. Goodnight, you two."

I used some of those hours that sleep still eluded me to make lists of people to inform about my situation, and things I had to take care of in regard to it. Like Dad mentioned, passwords and account numbers would have to be changed wherever possible. I spent a lot of the time studying the material I had brought home from work, too. It bolstered my confidence for the impending certification exam, plus it helped take my mind off of Sally long enough to catch a little rest before morning.

26

A ton of people were in the community college lot when I parked my car. I was comfortable enough so that I didn't have to look over my shoulder at every step to the building. I was happy to see my colleagues when I joined them in the meeting room. I think we were all still glowing from the day before. We greeted each other, and Jake said, "Good morning, Michelle." That was so much nicer than having a snarl with my coffee in the morning.

John was there in front of us with a big grin on his face. "Well, team BMW, you did it."

He keeps using that word team. Interesting…I certainly would not have considered us a team on Monday.

"As I told you yesterday, you exceeded expectations. Let me count the ways. You increased value for the customer by decreasing flow restriction, you reduced mass and weight when you eliminated the need for any attachment hardware, and you reduced the cost by 70%. Then you developed that idea even further when you listed all the benefits and non-recurring costs. I laid all this before Dean when he asked about our progress, and he was shell shocked to say the least. I don't think he believed me. After an uncomfortable silent pause he told me I must have missed understood your financial calculation. But enough about Dean…"

"Presentation Phase is next, team. I believe you were assigned and ready yesterday to gather the information that you'll need to work on for this phase today. You still have to come up with a detailed and clearly written value alternative for each idea that you had selected for further development. When you do present to management, there must never be an 'I don't know" response to any question asked, whether written or oral."

"Do we have to hike back to the office for this research, John?" asked Bob.

"Are you trying to get back to your desk again, Bob? Sorry, we've brought it all to you, here."

"Damn! Foiled again."

I saw Bob smiling behind his hand. I think he was actually enjoying the freedom of working away from the office.

"You will find yourselves supplied with process specifications, routings, assembly instructions, warranty documents, internal quality metrics, drawings, cost data, and everything else we could collect to be helpful for this phase."

"We've also created a standardized form to make it easier for you, and for whomever you present it to. You can document all recommendations here with written descriptions, reasons for justification, and everything I mentioned yesterday. You will need a summary page, too. Doug will pass out these forms to you now. Thank you, Doug."

With our redesign in mind, with which we hoped to surprise management, we eagerly attacked the forms, coming up for air only when John reminded us it was break time.

"You know where the coffee is by now, " he said.

Nobody argued.

On the way to the rear of the room, Bob tapped my shoulder. "Michelle, you know that mentoring situation we talked about yesterday? I've been mulling that over, and I think it could work. How about if I call Jake over now? There's no specific project as of yet, but it might work on a general basis for a while. What do you think?"

"That's perfect. I think it will help. Thank you."

"Okay, let's do it." He caught Jake's eye and motioned him over.

"Hey, Bob. What's up?" He glanced at me and back to Bob. "Is anything wrong?" he asked.

"No, as a matter of fact, everything's right. I've got a little job for you. It's really at Michelle's request. She says she would like your help, and I think it makes sense, at least for a while."

Jake turned to me, eyebrows raised. "You want my help?"

"If you don't mind, Jake, I could use a mentor. I've had so much thrown at me at one time. You've been here a good while, and know so much more. I'd appreciate it if you could just keep an eye on what I do and help me along."

"That would save me time, too, that I could use elsewhere," Bob said. "Will you do it?"

Jake scratched his head. "Well . . . uh . . . sure if you need me," Jake said to me.

I touched his arm. "Thanks so much, Jake. I promise I won't waste your time."

"You're welcome." He drank his complete cup of coffee down in almost one gulp, and went back for more.

Bob winked at me. "I guess that went well." He went back for his second cup.

John didn't ring a bell, but he did call us back from our morning break, ever mindful of Dean's deadline. We continued to work on the value alternatives through the afternoon to be sure they were accurate, clear and concise. It was hard to pull away from this project when it was time for lunch, and we knew there was so much more to do but John had told us throughout these meetings that we would do much better if we stoked our furnaces with nourishment -- and I thought I left my mother at home.

27

Without anyone saying anything, our feet turned toward Chip's restaurant. We headed there all together. I think we'd begun to consider it "our place."

"Gee, we've had really nice weather since the workshop began," I said to no one in particular.

"It's unusual for Chicago to have more than three days in a row like that. Wait! What was that? Drops?

"Oh no! I jinxed it!"

As of one mind, we moved faster, like a train picking up speed.

"So we can blame it on you, huh?"

I turned and looked up at Chip's smiling face. I felt smaller than I was, as I craned my neck for direct eye contact. With his six-feet-five frame, I almost couldn't see the balding top of his head. Some blonde hair showed around the back and sides -- or maybe some of it was grey. I never took notice before, and it was hard for me to tell now that he stood before me at his full height. His pleasant smile, though, drew my eyes back to his face. If someone were to ask me later what he looked like, that's what I would remember first.

"Sorry about that, Chip," I said.

"That's okay, as long as you bring back the sun."

It was just a few sprinkles to start. By the time we made it into the restaurant, it had become heavier.

"Whew, we beat that one," Chip said. The way we filed in, he wound up sitting next to me for lunch.

"So is anything new with that plane decompression? Did the Board hand in their findings?"

"Not yet, but you know those investigations take a while. Yesterday, I was told they think turbulence might be a factor, but they're still doing passenger interviews and going over the recordings. Chip, could our valve have had anything to do with it?"

"I doubt it could have caused the decompression, but maybe something happened to it afterwards as a result. I guess we'll have to wait and see."

"Are you comfortable again with travel? You sounded a little spooked there for a while."

"Oh, I don't even think about that anymore. Accidents can happen with anything, I suppose. Flying is safe, compared to all the other modes and faster too. Besides, I make enough trips. I might as well relax."

The food we ordered was served, and I had to take that first bite right away. I didn't realize how hungry value alternatives could make a person. We both tended to our food for a quiet minute or two, and I decided this was as good a time as any to say something about Sally and get it over with. I wasn't happy to talk about it.

"Chip, I have to tell you something. In fact I have to tell the whole staff. I'm having a bit of a stalker problem."

"What? You're kidding?"

"No, I'm quite serious, and the police want me to alert the office about her. She's a woman in her 60's. If anyone comes or calls, please don't give out any information about me or my where abouts. You're the first person I've told. I'd appreciate it. I think she's becoming dangerous."

"My God! Who is she? What does she want?"

I told him the story. He couldn't believe it any more than I could.

"Of course, I'll be sure to look out for her. That's terrible. You're telling everyone, you said?"

"Yes, the police were adamant about that."

"Maybe I can help with some of it."

"Thanks, Chip."

"Everybody through? Time to go," John called out. "And the rain stopped for us, too."

"Party pooper!" somebody said.

28

Back at the meeting room, we slipped into our
chairs, looking forward to building the Implementation Plan.
But we discovered we weren't quite ready for that. I thought
John was brave when he stood up to face us with the news.

"I know you are all anxious to move on at this point
and present your hard work to the executives. But when you
do that, you will be making a pitch. You will want to sell your
new design idea to them with logic and accurate valuation
that will be impossible for them to resist. Each phase of this
process needs to be perfect, and as I said before, with no
question left in their minds."

"Yes, Bob?"

"Are we doing the reviews individually, or is this to
be consensus like the FAST Diagramming?"

"I'm glad you asked. We're doing consensus. If we
all agree about the alternatives' performance assessments,
we're more likely to have the best and most accurate answers
to pass on to management, and your enthusiasm will be
contagious. It's important to check for errors, and I don't
mean typos; ensure narratives are complete; and that the
performance has been assessed properly. Keep in mind that
sometimes, when flaws are discovered, it's often possible to
compensate for them by an approach from a different angle."

All the forms that were collected were pretty
straightforward, and we spent the rest of the afternoon going
over them, one by one, remembering that, ultimately, our
credibility was at stake. When differences of opinions

occurred about the possibility of implementation or other factors, we didn't stop arguing and discussing them until a consensus was reached.

A shrill whistle from John, which I imagine he thought was the only way he could get our attention, stopped us short, like a factory whistle at closing time. It worked. We all knew what it was for, and somebody said, "Oh, no!"

"Sorry, you have to take your coffee break. I don't believe I had to say that. You people are something else." He chuckled.

"Forget the coffee, and let us continue, then," said Chip.

"I can't," John said.

"Why not?"

"It is written."

On that biblical note, everyone made a mass exodus to the coffee urn. We all returned in under ten minutes, and John just shook his head.

At day's end, we felt we had accomplished what we set out to do. We were careful not to rush it, and made sure our conclusions were well founded. We realized, though, that it would take at least part of the next day to finish it properly, including the Implementation Plan.

As before, we barely noticed that the day had melted away. This had been another great give-and-take session that I could add to the reasons I was happy I joined this company and this industry. This was not only a technical education but working with like-minded people who found interest, stimulation, and challenge here, as I did, created a sense of community. I felt that I belonged here, even in this short time, and that I was going to be able to become the engineer I wanted to be.

"Okay, team. Good job. Time to go," John said. "We do want the college to allow us to keep meeting here until we finish our project."

Still filled with a sense of achievement overall, everybody said their good nights and thanked John for his infinite patience.

"Yours, too," he said, "and don't forget, tomorrow is Implementation Plan day."

29

It was 5:30 p.m. I was in a hurry to leave. I had wanted to go to the library for a week now. I had put that on the back burner because of the craziness with Sally. I promised myself as well as my family that I would be cautious, but I was determined that she was not going to ruin my life. I called home to let my parents know that I might be a little late, so they wouldn't worry.

"I have a couple of things I need to check out at the library, Mom. . . .Yes, I'll be careful, and, yes, I'll be home before dark. If you and Dad get hungry, go ahead and eat. . . . I'll be fine, Mom. . . . What? . . .Have someone walk me to the car? Okay, I will. . . . I love you, too. Bye."

I was almost at the exit door of the building when Leland walked up behind me.

"Have a nice night, Michelle," he said.

"Oh, Leland, are you parked nearby?"

"Yes, a few cars down in the next row from here."

"My car is in the same section. Do you mind if I walk with you?"

"Of course not. Is something the matter?"

"Sort of. I have a problem."

"Another one?" He laughed. "Michelle, are you sure you don't need a keeper?"

"I'm beginning to think so, myself." I gave him a brief rundown about Sally, and what she looked like. As we walked to the cars, my eyes were everywhere.

"That's not funny," he said. "What are you doing about it?"

I explained the latest police intervention. "But it's just the beginning."

"You poor kid. I'm sorry to hear that. What can I do?"

"Thanks Leland. I haven't had a chance, yet, but I need to ask the staff not to give out any information about me or my where abouts. If it's business, I'll call them back. I happened to sit next to Chip at lunch, so he's the only I've told so far."

"I'll spread the word."

"That's so nice of you. Thanks a lot. Oh, there's my car. Thanks for the escort, too. See you tomorrow."

"Take care, Michelle."

With a wave, I got into the car while Leland was still there, and I hit the road. The library wasn't far from where my folks lived, so it was about the same twenty-minute ride. The days were just starting to grow longer, so there would still be plenty of light before 7:30P.M. I turned on a music station and caught a tribute to Michael Jackson. That lifted my spirits a bit. I always liked his music.

I reached the library and hurried in. I expected to be there a while, because I had some research to do. First of all, I wanted a good book on Value Analysis to supplement the workshop. Different sources sometimes explain things in different ways, and you can often pick up unexpected nuggets of information that can't be found elsewhere.

The second item I was after had to do with airplane incidents of decompression, what might have caused them, and how they were dealt with. I was sure that would require more time, since I would most likely have to do archive searches for articles.

I was happily into it, and almost finished, when I couldn't believe my eyes. I saw Sally across the room, smiling at me. And then she waved. Oh my God! How will I get home? My stomach came up into my throat. I stayed where I was for a minute. "Calm down," I told myself. "You have to think." When my breathing returned to normal, I pulled out my cell phone and called home.

"Hello, Mom? I'm still at the library -- and so is Sally. I don't know where she picked up on me. She must have followed me. Maybe she has that GPS enablement Dad was talking about. Listen, can you and Dad come and pick me up? . . . You're going to call the police? . . .For surveillance? Okay. Tell them to come without their sirens blaring. They might be able to catch her before she leaves. I'll wait inside at a table near the door. Bye."

I felt sure nothing would happen inside the library but I felt so small that the police were coming to protect me. I took the Value Analysis book and other material I had found to the checkout desk. I was also fairly confident that Sally was watching every move I made. But I could no longer see her. I sat down again at the table to wait.

It didn't take long for the police to arrive. There were two of them. I approached them and told them who I was. At that exact moment, I saw Sally slip out the door behind them. I yelled, "There she is!"

They spun around. "Come with us." They called back to me.

In the seconds it took us to get outside, Sally was nowhere in sight. We jumped in the squad car and searched the area for half an hour.

When it was clear we had lost her, we gave up. *How does she do that?* We returned to the library. Going home, one of the policemen drove my car behind the other policeman and me in the squad car. The whole way, we kept an eye out for Sally, but she never showed.

Before I got out of the car, Mom and Dad were out of their door. I knew what went through their minds, and I yelled to them, "Nothing happened. I'm okay." I let the police report the rest.

I thanked both the officers and went into the house. The day was kind of a downer. We had come close and missed her again. I thought I might feel better after I ate something. Lunch was my last meal, and it was about 8:00 p.m. when we reached home.

The officers went back to their car, prepared to stay a while, and Mom and Dad came into the house.

"You must be starved," Mom said. "Dad and I weren't hungry, so we had our soup and waited for you. Let's eat, and then you relax, young lady. You've had enough stress for one day."

"By the way, she called me at work. I was so embarrassed. I was in the middle of a meeting. I forgot to turn off the phone."

"You didn't answer it, did you?"

"No, but I had to leave the room to let it ring out, or it wouldn't go to voice mail. We'll have to listen to it after dinner. I haven't had a chance, yet."

Almost before I finished the sentence, the Sally phone rang. Mother gasped.

Dad said, "Oh my God! Don't answer!"

I was speechless. Mom wanted to hear both voice mails right away.

"Please, Mom, let's eat first. I don't want to lose my appetite."

The bowl of sautéed mushroom soup hit the spot for a starter. Mom had cut up the leftover brisket and produced a great beef stroganoff, served with noodles, peas and a leftover cobbler. I wouldn't want to insult the chef, but if I keep eating like this I'll never fit into a bikini.

With dinner over, we immediately went for the phone, our evening's entertainment. The first voice mail, which Sally had phoned in at work, was more threatening than the ones before it. You could tell she was angry that I didn't answer the call. The second message from an hour ago was escalating and even more frightening.

"Too bad we didn't get a chance to talk at the library, my dear," she said. "You would have learned something -- something important." Then she laughed. "You're not answering my calls, either. It just proves that I was right about you. Too bad! Now it's going to be a surprise. Wait for it!" She laughed that crazy laugh again and hung up.

I looked at my mother's face, and wished there were some way I could shield her from those calls. But she insisted on hearing them, even though they upset her.

"I told the detective I would call him if something else occurred. If you girls will excuse me, I'm going to do that right now."

"And I'm going take plates out to those poor men out there. I bet they are drinking cold coffee and eating stale donuts."

"I don't think giving them food is generally done, Mary."

"Well, I'm doing it. Maybe I'll start a new tradition."

Meanwhile, I posted the day's episodes on the log, two phone calls, an appearance . . . and a disappearance. I stared at the sheet and shook my head. I still couldn't believe this was happening. Then I set my jaw. *I'm not going to let her take over my life!*

"Michelle? Didn't you hear me, Princess?"

"Oh, no, Dad. Sorry."

"I just talked with the police. Your two lifeguards out there will be on watch for a while. He also said the airline gave him the information on Sally. They'll have everyone looking for her now."

"Tell me what they found out."

"Her name is Sally. They won't give me her last name. You hit her age on the nose; she's sixty-five years old. The police were able to check further. It appears she grew up in Chicago, but has been living alone in Sarasota."

"They said while she was still living with her family, she was diagnosed with paranoid personality disorder, and they placed her on medication. She seemed to improve, the police said, but then she refused any more meds. When her behavior became worse again, the family couldn't stand it and told her to leave. Then they lost track of her."

"Sad, huh, Dad?"

"Does seem that way. But with no one there for her, I guess she's worse now than she was then. Listen, I bought you another phone. Get this one going, and don't use the other one anymore. But leave it on and attached to e-mail."

"Okay, Dad, thanks." *If I get to work alive, I'll be looking forward to what lies ahead for me. I have to focus there. Now, that's something to dream about.*

30

The next day dawned bright and beautiful. It made you feel like there was nothing in the world that could go wrong. I decided to leave early, in order to check my computer at the office before going to the college. When I logged in, there were three messages, all from Sally. The first one said, "I found someone who thought it would be fun to help me punish you. Wait for it!" Two were a half hour later, fifteen minutes apart, both saying simply, "Wait for it!"

I felt nauseated, and my head started to spin. I called the police then and there. I told them who I was, and that I would send the e-mails to them. They said the officer in charge of the case would get it immediately. I hoped I would feel better by the time I arrived at the workshop.

When I reached the campus, there was a full lot again. But I understood that that didn't necessarily mean I was safe. I hurried to the building and on to the meeting room. I was the second one there. The first one was Jake.

"Good morning," he said. He sounded uncertain, as if he wasn't sure it was a good morning.

"Good morning to you," I said. "It's a nice day."

"Yes, it is." There was a nervous pause. "Michelle, will you have lunch with me today? I have to talk to you."

"Not if it's about shutting my mouth in meetings -- unless, of course, that's a new mentoring method."

His face dropped. "Well, it is partly about that, but not the way you think."

I'm not sure what I think. "Okay, Jake."

"Thank you."

John was the next one in. "Hi, there. It feels peaceful in here. It's a new day."

"Good morning," I said. "Yes, it is."

The group straggled in, now, with morning greetings. Everyone was in a good mood, in anticipation of the day and what lay ahead.

John waited for us to be seated. "Welcome back, gang. We still have a lot of work ahead of us before we present our solution to management for their approval. If you recall, we're going to finish up the value alternatives we have left to review. That will probably carry us until our break. After that, before we launch into the implementation plan, we'll discuss our sales pitch methods, or presentation. Let's get started."

I was inspired by the argument/discussion process because we expressed ourselves, new ideas erupted and new things were learned. What could be a better way to spend a couple of hours? Before we knew it, it was coffee time, and John was urging us out of our chairs. I'm sure we must have worn a path by now back to the coffee urn.

"Hey, Michelle, what in the world is going on with you?" That came from Randy. "It sounds like someone really put a hex on you coming into Chicago."

"What's he talking about?" Bob said to Jake.

I guess Chip and Leland didn't get around to everybody with the Sally story, yet, and before I knew it, I was surrounded by the team, including John. I repeated the whole thing, along with the request to not give out any information about me or my where abouts, and to say that I would return any business calls. They were all shocked and swore they would watch for her.

"Hey, I always have a camera with me. Photography is a hobby of mine. If you see her, I'll snap her picture for evidence." Doug said.

Others chimed in about Sally with, "Wow!"

"That's terrible!"

"Unbelievable!"

"Geez, Michelle, why didn't you tell me?" asked Bob.

"I wanted to. The police advised me to do this, and today is really the first chance I had."

"Well, I hope you remember you can come to me with anything. I'm always here for you -- and for the rest of the department, too."

"Thanks. That means a lot."

"Can't the police catch her, Michelle?" asked John.

"They're trying. They just found out her last name and a little of her history, and our house has more frequent drive-by surveillance now.

"I'm sorry to hear that," he said.

"Thank you, John. I have to be careful, that's all."

"All right, team. Are we through with the rest of the Alternative reviews?" asked John.

"We are," Bob said.

"Let's settle down, then, for some Presentation information. We'll make you all into master salesmen. This may sound elementary, but in order to do that, you have to know what you're selling, and to whom you're selling it. Now bear with me, because I'm going for something here. Randy, what about the first part? What are we selling?"

"We're selling improvements on our products."

"And that means we're also selling what? Anyone? Okay, I'll tell you. It's change. Not the kind that jingles in your pocket. It's the kind that many people resist. It's new ideas, new concepts, almost new anything. An awful lot of people do not like to be pushed out of their comfort zones. We have to convince them that change is a good thing. The next part, of course, is obvious. Chip?"

"We'll be selling our recommendations to management."

"And management are people like everyone else, right?" said Bob

A lot of chuckles and, "Yeah, right." was the response.

"Be nice, now," said John. "If you haven't already guessed by my rather roundabout way of getting to it, I'm saying that while some people celebrate change, others not only resist it but fight it. That means that we have to use every tool at our disposal to present a convincing argument. And that, folks, is the reason for all the forms and research you complained about recently. We have to think of answers to their questions before they think to ask them. But there's something more to it than information."

"Hey, John, when we're through with this session, will we be able to go door to door for Amway Products?"

"If you want to." said John.

"Go for it, Bob," somebody said.

"The 'something more' that I'm talking about," continued John, "is that the way you communicate your message makes a difference. In other words it's not what you say but how you say it that matters. If you sound cut and dried or bored management will be, too. Their attention may even drift. If you've never been in a sales position, you might want to consider practicing."

"So I suggest we take a little time before our afternoon coffee to do that. Break up in twos, then change partners and try to pitch an idea to each other. Sometimes you'll be in the management role; sometimes you'll be doing the selling. When you are taking management's position, think about whether you would be convinced; if you're pitching, put your heart into in to it. Use strong words. Get enthusiastic and even excited about the value alternative you're trying to promote. Speak in earnest. That can be contagious. Use the phrases that will make your listener believe that he has to consider the alternative you are recommending."

"But no fudging if there is even the slightest thing wrong with the concept you are trying to promote, or you will lose your credibility. Instead, you be the one to bring up the flaw and let it be known that you have a plan to mitigate that risk. Also, stay away from minute details. This presentation is not the venue for it. The purpose of this meeting is to get the approval to deploy the implementation action plan."

"Finally, do not forget, during your presentation, to give credit where it belongs: to Bob and his team for the original design and redesign; to Leland's new baseline concept developed from it; and then to the whole team."

"I believe that in your case, none of this should be difficult with the miracle your team has achieved. Again, I'm proud of you."

The roomful broke out in smiles and applause. "And on that note, let's go to lunch."

31

We always had an appetite after these sessions, it seems. So "our place" became almost an award for our efforts. By now the houses and buildings were comfortably familiar, and we even waved to some of the neighbors on the way. They became used to seeing us, too, I guess, because they waved back. I will miss that when we we're at our own building again.

"Hey, Michelle. Wait up."

It was Jake. He must have been one of the last ones out. Now I realized I didn't see him ahead. I stopped until he caught up, and we continued on to the restaurant.

"So are you going to go out and get a sales job on the side?" he asked.

"Not funny. I may need it to pay off my student loans. I thought John had some interesting points, though."

"Maybe, if you're the one who's going to make the pitch. That won't involve all of us, you know."

"I'm not sure how that works, but you know what? I'm thinking we can use some or all of that down the line in our business relations, anyway. We may discover later that it was valuable training."

"Hmmm. I never thought of that."

"Too bad they don't offer anger management classes with it."

I wouldn't have expected it of Jake, but he turned a lovely shade of red. "Look, I'm sorry, Michelle. That's one of the things I want to talk to you about."

"Okay, I . . . Oh, my God!"

"Michelle, what's the matter?"

"It's her! Jake, it's her! It's Sally! Over there, near the restaurant!"

"That's your stalker? That old lady? I see her. I'll get her. Stay here!"

He took off at a dead run, without a second thought.

"Jake, be careful! She might have a knife!" I yelled. *How stupid! How could I have just yelled that out loud. That was only a dream.*

Some of the guys were already in the restaurant. Three of them hadn't gone through the door, yet, and heard the commotion. They turned and took off after Jake.

"Oh, my God!" I said again. I was afraid for them.

I groped in my purse for my phone and called 911. "This is Michelle Jamison." I told them what was going on, and the location. "Is anyone nearby? Can you send someone right away? Please! . . .Yes, I'll wait outside the restaurant. Thank you."

I was still shaking when I hung up and saw Jake and the boys return. When they were close, I could see they were still breathing hard from the run. Jake was shaking his head.

"I'm sorry, Michelle. I don't know what happened. It's like she disappeared into thin air."

"I know. That's her specialty."

The others, Chip, Leland and Randy offered their apologies, too.

"But at least we caught a glimpse of her," Randy said. "So if we catch sight of her again, we'll recognize her. I didn't think fast enough, or I would have snapped a picture with my phone."

"Please don't apologize. I think it was wonderful that you all did this for me. Thank you. But, keep in mind, this woman could be dangerous. Maybe it's a good thing you didn't catch her."

The police drove up just then. I waved; they saw me and nodded. They parked in the middle of the street and came over to us. Jake looked at me with a question on his face.

"I'm sorry, Jake, I called them when you went after her. I didn't know what would happen, and the police said I should call them whenever there was an incident. You guys must be starved. Why don't you go in and have your lunch. I'll be along in a minute."

"You go ahead," Jake said to them. "I'll stay with Michelle. She should have someone with her."

"That's okay, Jake."

"No, I'm staying."

One of the two policemen who had arrived said, "Excuse me. Are you Michelle Jamison?"

"Yes, I am."

"Do you want tell us what happened?"

I went through the story from the beginning as briefly as I could. I could probably set it to music before this whole Sally thing was over. I had a hunch this wouldn't be the last time I'd be telling this tale.

"If you'll get into the squad car, we'll drive around and see if we can find her."

"That wouldn't work, officer. I didn't know how that chase would end, but we tried that before with the police. We drove around for half an hour and never saw her. Besides, this is my lunch hour, and I'm going to have to get back to work. Thank you for coming out."

"Yes, ma'am. We'll make the report. Call us again if anything happens."

Jake waited for them to leave. "Say, there's still time for lunch, Michelle. How about it?"

We went in after the first of the group had already been served, and, of course they had saved room for the rest of us. But, as in Bob's case, Jake managed to find us a table a little away, which raised a few eyebrows at the team table.

"Everything okay?" Leland called.

"Fine, Leland, and thanks again for the support."

Jake called the waitress over. "We're running kind of late, now. Sorry to ask, but can we have our orders pretty fast?"

"Sure. What'll you have?

"Would two burgers be okay, Michelle?"

"Perfect. They're good here."

"Got it," the waitress said. "Coming right up."

It was obvious that he was anxious for her to walk away, so that he could get what had been bothering him off his mind.

It took him a bit of throat clearing to get going. "Michelle, I want to apologize."

"But why . . . ?"

"Please, let me finish. This isn't easy for me." He picked up his spoon and started tapping it nervously on the table.

More throat clearing. "Michelle, I'm thirty years old. I put myself all the way through school working part-time jobs until I got my Engineering degree. Then I started the job search. After a lot of interviews and being hired by and leaving two different companies, I landed here, and for the first time in my life, I felt as if I'd found a home. Then you came on the scene, and, Michelle, I was positive you were hired to replace me. I was desperate. I was fighting for my professional life."

Jake, you must have known that wasn't even rational. Why in the world would they replace you with your experience and track record, with someone like me, fresh out of school with no practical experience at all?"

"I do know, but -- and I've never said this to anyone -- it's my stupid lack of self-confidence, and I apologize for the way I treated you. I only hope you forgive me."

"I forgive you as long as you didn't succeed in getting me fired and destroying me professionally. Besides I have to forgive my mentor," I said with a smile. "You know, Jake, maybe we can help each other."

"Friends?"

"Friends." I offered my hand for him to shake. To my surprise, he didn't let it go right away.

"Michelle, thank you for understanding."

Out of the corner of my eye, I noticed our group getting up to leave and checking us out. John turned around and called, "Lets go, you two."

"Oh, my gosh! I never noticed the waitress brought the food, did you?"

"Oh, no! Jake started to laugh. "We'd better have them wrapped to go. We can eat them at afternoon break. I'm not hungry, anyway, are you?

"Not really. I can wait until then, but won't the others wonder?"

"Let them eat donuts."

32

Jake and I ran out of the restaurant, laughing at ourselves as we hurried to catch up with the gang.

"Forget to eat? Who does that," I said. And we started laughing all over again.

The team entered the building ahead of us, but we weren't far behind. We discovered the bags we were carrying were too fragrant with our burgers-to-go to bring to our seats, so we left them behind the coffee urn.

Jake whispered to me, "We should have put our names on them, like lunch bags at grammar school."

I tried to smother a giggle, but didn't do a very good job of it. I managed to straighten out my face, but when I looked around, I noticed eyebrows were raised again. I thought John would have a comment, but he didn't flick an eyelash. He waited until he had our attention.

"Before you left for lunch," he said, "we talked about the presentation to management and having a little practice session. So let's try it and see what good sales people you are."

"Remember to be informal and relaxed. You won't be giving a lecture. Talk from your heart as you would to a friend, with real pauses and honest expression, so that what you say won't become one run-on sentence. Enjoy."

Leland, in the chair next to me, said, "Want to give it a try, Michelle?"

"Sure," I said.

"It sounds like fun. You want to start?"

"Okay," he said. "This isn't the real me, you know. I've never sold anything."

"That's fine. Neither have I. We could both use the practice."

Leland started out with a lot of "um's" and "er's" at first, but soon began to smooth out and pick up steam. I helped him with what I remembered about presentation skills, and then it was his turn to help me.

John let us know when fifteen minutes were up each time, and we changed partners. It began to feel like the fifteen-minute dating game. I must say, though, for those of us unfamiliar with selling anything, even a theory, it was worthwhile. And as I told Jake at lunch, the experience could be useful in other business situations.

Before we knew it, John was saying, "It's time for your break, team. If anyone is in the middle of a pitch, finish it up. And, just a suggestion, but if you would like to have more practice, try it at home in front of a mirror."

Jake and I looked at each other. We both had the same thought, our by now cold hamburgers. As if on cue, we made a run for it. I made sure he beat me to the urn. I didn't want to damage that delicate ego any further.

Bob watched our mad rush and said, "Now that's what I call hungry! Hey, how come you two are privileged? I hope you brought enough to share with everybody."

"It's our lunch, Bob. We forgot to eat it, and it was time to get back."

"You forgot to eat! That must have been some conversation. I hope you recorded it."

"No, but we did clear up some issues."

"Are things resolved between you?"

"They are, Bob. We're good."

Bob looked heavenward, smiled and said, "Thank God."

We got plenty of teasing from the others as we devoured our burgers. But talk became serious when the guys expressed concern about the Sally problem.

"Michelle, at the end of the day, do not go to your car alone. One of us will walk with you every day until she's caught," said Doug.

"Yeah," said Randy, "and you can be sure we're all going to be on the lookout for her."

Doug and Randy's eyes were narrowed, and their jaws were set. Both their expressions said that, in no uncertain terms, they meant business. In spite of their five-foot-ten heights, receding hairlines (Doug's very receding), and paunchy middles (Randy's very paunchy), their demeanors left no doubt they could be superheroes to be reckoned with when pushed. I was sure that Doug with his red hair and mustache and Randy with his dark hair and handlebar mustache would make a tough duo to behold.

Leland said, "Remember what I told you. If you run into any trouble at all, no matter what it is, call me."

All the rest seconded everything that was said.

Jake simply said, "You can count on me."

I was overwhelmed. This group had become like a second family in a very short time. "I don't know what to say, guys. Thank you so much, all of you."

John cleared his throat. Sorry, people, but I'm afraid we have to get back to it. It's time to tackle the Implementation Plan.

33

"This, team, is the last leg of this fascinating journey we've been on together, the Implementation Plan. First of all, each Value Alternative that has been accepted will require a plan for implementation. This may sound repetitious, but I can't emphasize enough that these people you have pitched to, your executives, must be assured in every way that the changes you've convinced them to go along with can and will be made smoothly and properly. Again, change is the key word here. That is what the Implementation Plan is all about. But a strategy for that change is useless if the company can't implement it effectively."

"I bet that means more forms," Jake said.

"You got that right," answered John. "Man's best business friend. It's worth the effort. Believe me. To many people, things seem more believable when they're written down on paper – especially if they've been well researched. It offers a means to check back for thoroughness and clarity."

John took us through the specific forms we would need to make our case. "You're all taking notes, aren't you?"

Everybody mumbled something I assume was "yes."

"To begin with, you will have narratives among your papers, where you need to give your rationale for recommending your alternatives, and you must deliver that message clearly. What management will want to know, and what your paperwork will reflect with well-researched accuracy, is how, in all ways, changes will impact the model currently in production."

"Cost, of course, is a major factor. Remember, we want to show the alternative will increase the profit for us at the same time it retains quality and meets the needs of the customer. How will it change the cost of production, time and labor? How have the materials changed?"

"What about the time impact? Will it shorten the time in assembly, packing and delivery? From what you tell me I believe it will even eliminate installation jobs on the airplane. By how much, in each case, and why? Are there fewer parts and fewer repeated functions? Exactly what are the part and function changes? Are the changes major or minor?"

"Are there down sides? If yes, be sure they're mentioned. Name them and describe them without too much minute detail. And, folks, that goes for any of your descriptions. If management wants even more detail (and we will give them enough) we can always supply it later. But we don't want to lose their attention by throwing too much at them at once. The purpose of the presentation is to get buy-in to move to the deployment phase. As to the negative factors, be prepared to let them know what can be done to fix them, what it would cost in terms of money and time to do that."

Finally, tell them how the changes and the accepted alternatives will be integrated into the project, and what will be affected by it in the system. Then hand it in to management, along with the spreadsheets and design proposals.

"When do we make this presentation, John?" asked Leland.

"We've got a weekend coming up, so it'll be next week, except for Dean. He wants to see the results as soon as they're ready. We've got a lot to do."

Getting ready for the scrutiny of management, we were spurred on by all the work we had already done over the past few days. And every one of us was so proud of the outcome, we were anxious to show it off. We went to work. After we finished, including all the benefits and non-recurring costs that we listed, John laughed when we told him we thought our implementation plan was a thing of beauty.

"I think we ought to replace the graphic designs in the office with it. What do you say?" said Bob.

"We'll see if management thinks so, too, when you do the presentation next week," said John. "But between you and me, I wouldn't worry. I'll lay a copy of this on Dean's desk right away. He'd never last until next week without seeing it. He can get the silent movie today and the presentation on Monday."

"Now I hope I won't be spoiling all this when I remind you about your AVS certification exam. Dean is anxious that you take it. Besides it never hurts to have another certification and CEU to your credit. I wish you all the best. You have two hours to complete the exam."

On Monday I never thought we would all be sitting here taking this exam. By all the negativity in the air I thought I might be here alone. The test was not so tough, at least so far. I guess John prepared us well throughout the week.

"We are going to be kicked out of here in about an hour. When you have completed your exam you are free to leave. Have a good weekend, team, and get a good rest. After your performance this week, I have to say you earned it."

"Hold it! Before you leave, who has 'Michelle duty' today.?"

"Now, really!" I said. I thought he was kidding at first.

"I've got it, John," Jake said. "We're going to figure out a schedule. I'm taking the first shift."

"I don't believe this," I said. "Jake, this is embarrassing. Aren't we taking this mentoring thing a little too far?"

"Don't feel that way, Michelle. It'll keep us from worrying that you don't have protection while that nut is running around. Like you said, she could be dangerous."

"I agree," said John. " Michelle. Let them do it."

"I guess I can't say no when you're all so great. Thank you." Now they were embarrassed and mumbled their "good nights" out the door.

"Have a good weekend," I called after them. "See you Monday."

"Ready?" Jake asked. "Let's go."

"Good night, John," we both said.

"Good night. And, by the way, I'm awfully glad you two patched it up."

34

Things had pretty much straightened out at work, but I still had Sally to worry about. Even though Jake was at my side, my eyes were everywhere as we walked to my car. Jake, too, was scanning the area, but didn't see a reason for alarm.

"Where did you park? Nearby?"

"It's right next to yours"

"Jake, you guys don't have to do this. It's an imposition."

"We do, and it's not. So no more discussion about that, okay?"

"Well, okay. Thank you again. Our team did great, didn't we?"

"Yeah, we did . . . You, too. Nice going, Michelle."

"Thanks, Jake. Well, I should go. We're here."

Jake held out his hand to take the keys from me to unlock the car, his other hand on the door handle.

"Go ahead. Open it. I'm looking forward to seeing this." Sally chuckled deep in her throat.

Both of us jumped. The sudden sound of the raspy, hag voice (it didn't sound like that when I first met her) shook both of us. It was as though she had materialized out of thin air, in the same way she had disappeared before.

She rose between the two cars next to me, just the other side of Jake's. I was startled, and fragments of my dream flashed across my mind.

Her smile was evil. Even though she was several feet away we could smell her. She reeked of body order and her breath was like a dirty ashtray. She said, "That's a nice car, Michelle. My helper thought so too. But be careful when you start it up. It would be a shame to ruin it. Repairs are expensive, you know." Then she laughed that raspy laugh again that sounded like a witch stirring her cauldron.

Whatever happened to that nice, frightened older woman who asked to change seats with me on the plane? She mutated into a different creature. Even her appearance was different. I thought she might have been staying with her Chicago relatives, but she clearly has been living on the street. Her clothes were beginning to look ragged and a little soiled, and her grey hair was no longer combed and cared for. She was a vision for Halloween. All that was needed was a pointed black hat and a wart on her nose.

Jake stopped with his hand in mid-air, holding the key.

"I'd better leave, Jake. I'll take the key."

"Wait, Michelle." He pulled me back gently by the shoulders. "Get away from the car."

"What are you doing? Are you crazy?"

"No, but she is. Didn't you hear her? I think she might have done something to it."

"Before I could stop him, he got down and rolled under it. Then I heard a low, slow whistle. When he came back out, he was grim. "Looks like you're going to be late tonight, Michelle."

"What is it, Jake. What did you see?"

"Just stay back. I'm calling the police. It's a pipe bomb!"

"Oh, my God! Is it ticking?"

"No," he said as he pulled out his phone, "but it's wired to the car. She said she wanted you to turn on the ignition, right?"

He dialed 911 and then stayed with me to wait for the police. Sally had melted away again.

By then, I was on my phone with my parents. I
hated to make another crisis call to them, but I figured they'd
be more worried if I didn't show for dinner than if I let them
know what was going on.

"Oh, no! Are you all right?"

I barely got the words, "Yes, Dad" out of my mouth,
when Mom chimed in with, "We'll be right over. We're
leaving now."

Of course, I was sure they weren't going to sit by the
phone for more news once they heard. Not my parents. I
smiled and shook my head and watched for them.

As soon as I put down the phone, Jake told me,
"The police said that when Sally is caught, she's going to be
in deeper trouble than ever, Michelle. The bomb squad will
notify the FBI about this, since it's on community college
property. It seems the police have a liaison with the Bureau
of Alcohol, Tobacco and Firearms, anyway."

"What do you think the police will do?"

"I'm not sure, but I heard they have a bomb truck
that carries special equipment for explosives. They may have
that with them when they get here."

As if on cue, a squad car pulled into the lot and
turned off the siren. A white truck followed and parked
nearby. Several police jumped out of the squad and
immediately dispersed a small crowd that had gathered. At
the same time, a policeman spotted us standing where we had
parked.

"Are you Jake Evans?" he asked.

"Yes, sir. This is the car I called about. It's wired
underneath, and we have reason to believe it will explode on
ignition."

"We'll talk to you more about this later, Mr. Evans.
In the meantime, we will evacuate this building, and I have to
ask you both to leave, as well.

"This didn't look like a huge bomb to me, sir. Is it
really necessary to evacuate the whole building?" asked Jake.

"I'm afraid so. We don't know how stable this is. If it were to explode before we could get it out of here, we have no way to predict what could happen, especially with its placement in a car. The concussive force alone might knock down a wall or a building. Then you've got a car exploding with all types of shrapnel -- chunks of metal, glass, whole doors or windows, or other whole parts that can be fired in any direction. Plus distance and size are factors, too, which makes it hard for us to judge. The destruction would be too horrible to property and victims to describe. We don't play guessing games with this, Mr. Evans, and we don't take any chances."

"Wow!"

"The longer we wait, the more iffy it gets, and I see the evacuation is about complete. So if you'll provide us with your information and take your family to safety, we'd all feel a lot better. We'll call you before we come to take your statement at your address."

"We don't live together." Jake said.

"Then maybe it would be easier for you both to come to the station. When we call, just let us know."

"Thank you, officer," I said.

"Are you okay, Ma'am? You look pale."

"Yes, I'll be fine."

He turned to Jake. "You'd best take her home where she can calm down. We'll take care of this and call you."

As I looked around, people had already poured out of the building, and the lot had emptied out, too. The squad seemed to have organized the exodus very well. That's when I saw my parents. I waved and went over to them, while Jake gave the officer our information.

"Are you all right?" Mom asked again, as if she didn't believe me when I spoke to her on the phone. I know she needed to hear it again.

"I'm okay, Mom, thanks to Jake, but we have to leave here while they work on the car."

Jake joined us, and I put my arm in his. "Mom, Dad, this is Jake Evans."

"How do you do," Jake said.

"Aren't you the young man who was giving my daughter a hard time?"

"Dad, not now!"

"I'm afraid so, sir. I'm sorry. It was a misunderstanding."

My father looked at my face and took my cue.

"Hmmph!" he said and turned away.

"Jake, I don't know how to thank you. You saved my life."

Dad turned back on his heel. "Is it true?"

"Yes, Dad, it is."

My father put out his hand and warmly shook Jake's. "Apology accepted! Thank you for saving my little girl. We can talk about that other nonsense later."

Mom, always a little more emotional, rushed over to Jake, kissed him on the cheek and gave him a bear hug. "Thank you, thank you," she said.

To say Jake was surprised was an understatement. He managed to say, "You're welcome, but I just happened to be there."

My Dad, calmed down by then, said, "Thank God you were!"

The policeman Jake had left caught my eye and waved us on.

"We have to leave now." I said.

"Okay. Let's go, Jake," Mom said. She grabbed Jake's other arm and we walked to the cars.

35

"Are you expected anywhere for dinner?" Dad asked Jake.

"No sir, I'm not."

"How about your parents?"

"They're gone a long time, now. I live alone."

"I'm sorry to hear that. But it's settled, then. You'll have dinner with us." Insisted mom.

"Oh, no ma'am. I couldn't impose."

"Listen, you're looking at an incredible cook right here, and tough, too. I wouldn't argue with her if I were you. I've never won an argument with my wife, yet."

Jake glanced sideways at me. I nodded and smiled.

"Thank you, it'll be a pleasure," he said.

Our car is parked down a way. We'll bring it back here and leave together."

"I'll keep Jake company in his car, Dad, and we'll follow you."

We were about to head out when one of the officers, notebook in hand, called me over.

"Before you leave, I need just a little more information about this stalker. The file is in our office, of course, but this could help us now."

"Okay."

"Ms. Jamison, have you had any violent contact with her before?"

"No. She's threatened, but nothing actually happened."

"How long ago was her last threat?"

"Not long. She's been contacting me in some form almost every day."

"Then I don't have to tell you that the way she has escalated, you'll be in constant danger. I see that you've already got our police increasing patrols by your house. Please be sure that whenever you are out and about, you are never alone."

He was mistaken if he thought that was going to make me feel better. I was thirsty for any new information, and he had nothing much to tell me. He did say they found her family here, who said they hadn't seen her in years, since they asked her to leave. That's so sad. If she had someone to advocate for her in the past, maybe she wouldn't be in the state she's in now.

Jake and I got into his car to wait for Mom and Dad, explaining to the officer that we would leave in a minute, as soon as my parents drove by for us. He nodded okay.

I sat next to Jake, saying nothing, my mind a long way off.

"What are you thinking?" he asked.

"About functions and how Sally's whole life system malfunctioned.

"What do you mean?"

"We've been so immersed in functions and value. It strikes me that it applies to life, too. We all have our functions that relates to everyone around us. We depend on each other for the function that each of us provides, whether it's to love, support, to take care of each other, to spur one another on to better things, and it all adds up to building a system -- a life system. You know, I believe we could actually do a FAST Diagram based on human lives. John even said it: 'Everything has a function.' It doesn't apply to products and inanimate things alone, Jake. It's life and the whole world we live in."

Jake didn't say anything; he just looked at me, and I heard, "Whew!" After a minute, he said, "You know you can't help her, Michelle. She's too far gone and too dangerous. I hope you won't be traveling around by yourself when you get your car back. From what I've seen, Sally is capable of anything."

"That's what that policeman just said to me. But what choice do I have, Jake? Hire a bodyguard?"

Jake raised his eyebrows and shrugged.

"You're kidding! I wouldn't be able to do anything I came to Chicago for, except go to work and come home. And that's not acceptable."

"What is it you want to accomplish, Michelle?"

"First of all, I still haven't had a chance to work on that flight decompression situation, and we're almost through with the value analysis workshop. I thought I might at least get in some research on that, and maybe even some interviews with a few of our people and others who deal with it. Plus if I'm lucky, maybe the board will issue their final report by then.

"Gee, Michelle, I can help with that, if you let me. It would be great if we solved the puzzle together, and it would be fun having a partner."

"Thanks, Jake, I'd like that, but it still doesn't help the protection issue."

"What else is on your agenda? Can I ask?"

"It's not that big a deal, but I'd like to attend some lectures and conferences, not only concerning our industry, but humanities and the arts, too. This city is a treasure full of almost anything you want to learn, see, or hear about. And, Jake, I'm here! I want to be able to take advantage of that."

"And you can't do that with a bodyguard?"

"Jake, could you? I'd feel like an idiot. Everyone would wonder who in the world I am."

"How about an escort? Would you consider that?

"Are you offering?"

"I'm available . . . with a little advance notice, of course."

"Why would you do that?"

Jake considered that for a moment. "Partly as an apology for being a jerk."

I laughed at that. "Well, maybe a misguided jerk. You're so nice to offer. Let me think about it. Hey, there are my parents."

They honked and moved in place to lead us. "We'd better go."

We waved to the cop as we drove out.

36

Driving back to the house was uneventful, thank goodness. After the day's goings on, it was good to see home turf again. We waited for Dad to pull into the garage; Jake drove up the driveway and parked. He saluted the police on their duty watch; they smiled and nodded.

Mom, with her usual sense of organization, had made dinner earlier in the day. She wasn't even concerned about an extra person at the table, because there was always more than enough. The word, "portion" was not in her cooking vocabulary.

"Make yourselves comfortable on the patio, guys. I'll go in and get things going. I'll have cold drinks out here in a minute," she said.

Mom disappeared inside, and, much to my chagrin, Dad started his "if you're going to date my daughter I want to know more about you" routine. He didn't get very far because I changed the subject in a hurry.

"Dad, when you called the police last time, was there anything new? The officer at the lot today didn't have much to tell me, except they found her family, but not her."

"Oh, yes. The cop I spoke with asked me if you've kept an incident log. Remember, we talked about that. I think it was about the time you had that nightmare, or maybe a couple of days later."

"Yes, I have been keeping a log. But it occurred to me that I forgot to put down the policeman's name and badge number when I reported one of the e-mails. Do you think they might have a record of the call? Maybe I should check and see."

"I think they would. This officer mentioned a Civil Restraining Order, too. I guess we should have already applied for one. We'd better do that now. I believe we'll have to go to court, but I'm not sure if it will be civil or criminal court. I'll talk to a lawyer."

"Mr. Jamison, why bother doing that if Sally can't be served?"

"The log, restraining order, police reports, and any relevant documents we may have, the police told us, can potentially be used as evidence, even if it was obtained without her knowledge – that is if they ever catch her."

"I'm so sorry you and Mom had to be bothered with all this, Dad."

"Nonsense. We're just sorry this had to happen to you. Don't you know, princess, what happens to you happens to us. We will always be there for you. Your brothers, too."

"Oh, my God! I've been so busy, I keep forgetting about that."

"Is that bad?" Jake asked.

"They just can't get over the fact that I'm their 'little sister.' They're libel to form a posse and go after Sally themselves."

"Maybe that's a good thing."

"Dad!"

Jake and Dad thought that was funny. I didn't. Mom heard all the laughter just as she came out with a pitcher each of ice tea and lemonade, and glasses.

"What did I miss?" she said.

Jake jumped up and took the tray from her.

"Hey, don't spoil her."

"As if you never did!" I reminded Dad.

"Who are those two extra glasses. for?" asked Jake

"The police," she said, and promptly poured ice tea and took the glasses to their car.

"There will be food, soon," she told them.

"You don't have to do that, Mrs. Jamison," I heard them say.

"It's okay. No problem."

Mom sat down with us, and we sipped our drinks. It was getting toward the day's end. We inhaled the late-day smell of moist grass, and the cicadas began their song. We took turns talking about what we saw ourselves doing by next year, and that was okay, because it wasn't centered on me. Then we talked about Jake's volunteering to be my sometime escort and protector and why he was willing to do that. That was okay with my parents, because it was about me.

Mom rang her verbal dinner bell, we drained our glasses, Jake gathered them and carried the tray indoors, where those wonderful kitchen aromas lurked.

"No wonder Michelle is so anxious to get home for dinner all the time. What smells so good?" Jake asked.

All Mom would say was, "You'll see."

37

We took our seats around the table. I got up to help her bring everything in. The menu (and I do mean menu) consisted of a large roast stuffed chicken, spinach loaf casserole, and small, round roasted onion potatoes. It all went down easily with a glass of chardonnay.

Jake was impressed. "Excuse me, but are you celebrating a holiday? This is like a feast. You didn't know I was coming. Do you eat like this all the time?"

"Almost," said Dad. "She can't help herself. She likes to cook and I like to eat. We're a perfect match.'"

"Are you kidding?" asked Jake.

"Yes," said Dad, grinning.

"Aw, go on, you two. It's simple, basic food."

Jake shook his head. "The best I've had in a long time."

Then the phone rang. It was the wrong one, the one we don't answer. We all just looked at each other. Fear crept into the room on cat's feet. Jake said, "Isn't someone going to answer the phone."

"The only number Sally has is the one we don't pick up, Jake. The police told us to get a second phone, and let her messages go to voice mail on this one. That way we don't have to respond to her. They said response of any kind incites her further. We'll listen to it later," I said.

We went on with our dinner and enjoyed it. But it was a lot quieter than when we began. My folks learned a bit more about Jake. I think the wine opened him up.

"How old were you when your parents died?"

"Dad!" I screamed.

"It's okay, Michelle. I was nineteen. It was difficult. You know, hard as I've tried, I can't remember feeling the warmth of a loving family that I've felt here. Even when they were alive, they always had money problems and both of them were always away, working hard. I'm sure they loved me. After all, I was their only child. But they never had time. And if they did, they were just too tired."

I looked at Mom. She was practically in tears. I know she would have loved to give him a hug again and tell him everything would be all right. Instead, she cleared her throat, and since we had finished dinner by then, she figured this was a good time to clear things away.

"Why don't you all go in the other room. I'll be in shortly. I want to hear that phone call."

"I'll help you, Mom."

I piled some of the dishes together and carried them into the kitchen. It always felt good when just the two of us were together for girl talk. This time Mom stopped me and put her hand on mine.

"Michelle, I want to tell you something about when you apologized for 'bothering us'. I just want you to know that you have our love and our hearts, and nothing about you is a burden. And one of your functions in life will be to carry our love for you and pass it on to someone who will raise your existence to something wonderful."

Mom kissed me, and I couldn't speak. *Now my mother is talking about functions?*

"Now let's get done here and listen to that awful woman," Mom said.

Between the two of us, we finished pretty quickly, with dishes in the sink, and the leftovers put away.

"He's a nice boy," Mom said. "He just had a rough start."

"I know, Mom. I know."

"Are you girls ready?" Dad called from the den. "It's getting late. Jake wants to leave soon."

"We're coming," Mom called back.

It took another minute, and we joined them.

"Okay?" Dad asked.

"Go ahead, Bill."

Sally's raspy voice came through loud and clear. "Michelle, you've been ignoring me again, and I don't like that. You're not answering your phone. That makes me angry. Believe me, you don't want to make me angry. It looks like I may have to pay you a visit at your house instead of your car. Good-bye, Michelle."

"Oh, my God!" said Jake. "Is there anything I can do?"

"You've done a lot, already!" Dad promptly picked up a phone to call the police. "Don't forget to log this, Michelle. I'll get the name and badge number for you."

"I'd better get going," Jake said. "Mr. and Mrs. Jamison, I can't thank you enough. This was one of the nicest times I've had for a while."

"We enjoyed having you, Jake, and thank you again for saving Michelle's life." Then he got that hug from Mom, after all.

"Words aren't enough," said Dad. "Drive safely, now."

"I'll call you tomorrow, if it's okay with you, Michelle."

"That's fine, Jake. Have a good night."

38

I awoke early Saturday morning, intent on running off some of Mom's dinner. I dressed in my running clothes, laced up my shoes, and away I went out the side door. That was the closest exit to the route I planned to take. I wanted to enjoy this beautiful day, stretch out my muscles and take in gulps of fresh air as I ran toward the corner at Hawthorne Avenue and made a right turn, heading south toward Lincoln Park. It was a few blocks to Belmont and Sheridan for another left, and then a straight shot to the Harbor. It was barely light, and way too early for any bicycle traffic on the path. Even better. I hit my stride on the lake front path and just kept going. It felt good to be active again. I ran every day at school, but didn't have a chance since I've been home.

What's the function of running? Relieve Pressure? Improve Health? Enjoy Life? I've been brainwashed. Everything is a function to me now.

A little farther south took me to the Theater on the Lake. I was about two blocks away from that point, when I saw a figure standing next to a bike. I didn't think anyone else would be out on the path as early as I was, but after all, it was Saturday. I couldn't tell if it was a man or a woman, but that didn't ring any particular alarm bells.

As I came closer, I realized it was a woman wearing an Army helmet. I was still about a half a block away when she began to look familiar, and my brain woke up. I slowed to a stop and looked around me. Still no bike or runner traffic; no one anywhere in view. When I looked back again, she had disappeared.

Was I seeing things? I continued on at a slow trot. When I turned the corner by the theater, she sprang out in front of me, arms out to the sides. It was Sally. I screamed. There was nothing I could do. Even if I ran, all she had to do was hop on the bike. Fear paralyzed me. I had no choice but to face her. *I thought I heard a car, but I didn't see anything. It must have been wishful thinking.*

"How did you know I would be running out here?" I gasped.

"I didn't, dear. I don't have a car, you know. I just got this bike. I was heading toward your house. I got lucky. Whadyaknow!"

"Listen, Sally. I didn't abandon you. I found out where they were taking you, and as soon as I got to Chicago, I called that hospital. They said they were keeping you overnight, and that you were fine." *I was sure I heard a car.*

"You're a liar! Then why didn't you stay in Orlando with me until I got out?"

"Because they said you were okay, and my family was expecting me. Plus I had to go to a new job the next day."

"I don't believe you. You didn't care. My own family didn't care. Nobody cares. Somebody's got to pay."

Sally shook her arm a little and something slipped out of her sleeve.

"Oh, my God! No!" It was the same knife I saw in my dream.

She raised her arm over her head, the blade pointing toward me. I screamed. "No, Sally! Don't! Stop! You're making a mistake!"

A car's brakes screeched, and all I saw was a blue blur. The next thing I knew, Sally was on the ground, and the cop was putting handcuffs on her hands behind her back. She kicked and screamed, "I'll get you! You'll see! I'll get you! You'll pay for this! The other cop with him grabbed her, too, and they both put her in the car's secured back seat. She didn't stop shrieking and banging the cage with her cuffs.

The policeman turned to me. "Are you all right, ma'm?" He took a handkerchief out of his pocket, picked up the knife and reached for an evidence bag in the car.

"A little hysterical, but I guess I'm okay, thanks to you."

"We called for backup. You don't want to get in our car. Not with her in there!"

"Will you call my folks, too?"

"Sure. They're the ones who found you missing. They noticed your running shoes weren't there, so they had an idea where you'd be. We were doing surveillance outside your house and came to look for you. We didn't see you leave."

"I'm sorry. I used the side door. I didn't think."

Another car pulled up behind the police. Dad jumped out. "Princess!"

"I'm okay, Dad. Just shook. I know what you're going to say."

"Right. What were you thinking? You should never have gone off by yourself. I told you; the police told you . . ."

"I know, Dad." I prepared myself for the lecture all the way home, and was happy to hear it. I couldn't stop shaking.

He phoned my mother as soon as we got into the car. I heard her say, "Oh, thank God," and then she burst into tears. Of course, I was grabbed as soon as I walked in the house, and Mom almost squeezed the life out of me. But I didn't object to that, either.

"Just think," she said. "You won't ever have to worry about Sally again."

"I'll think about that later, Mom, after I get over this. I'm sure I'll be fine tomorrow."

"Speaking of tomorrow," she said, finally releasing me, "Jake called. He was upset when he heard what happened. I told him you were okay, and to call back Sunday."

"Thanks. I think I'll go and rest now."

"Have a cup of hot tea, first. It'll relax you."

39

I slept later than usual the next day. I woke up about 11:00 a.m. to the aroma of coffee and pancakes. That was one of Mom's breakfast specialties. There were "good mornings" and hugs from both Mom and Dad.

"How do you feel?" Dad asked.

"Better," I said, "and hungry."

Like magic, my plate was heaped and my cup was full.

"Are you planning to stay around today?" Mom asked.

"I think so, unless I go to the library. Of course you would have to drive me, if you wouldn't mind, Dad. I'd like to find more material on airplane decompression. We also have a presentation tomorrow at work, and I want to look over those papers again."

"Why don't you call Jake and see if he can go with you, Michelle."

"I can't bother him, Mom. I'm sure he has things he has to do."

"You know, Princess, the police want you both to go in and sign a statement, anyway. Are you're up to it today? Dad was talking to them, and they said you will have to testify, as well, unless they find her unfit to stand trial. It seems to me there's a good chance of that, though."

"Maybe I will call Jake. We might as well go in and get that statement business over with. They said they would call us, but I would like to put all this behind me as soon as possible."

"You should log in this last incident, too," Dad said. "Keep the phone that has her messages on it together with it. And don't forget the e-mail messages you printed out. The police will want all of that for evidence."

"Oh, that's right. I'll take it with me when I go in. Thanks for the reminder."

"There goes the phone. I'll get it," Mom said.

"Hello? . . . Good morning, Jake . . . Yes, she's here . . . She's good. Just a minute. It's for you, Michelle."

"Hi Jake . . .No, I'm okay . . . No, I'm really fine . . . Was it a surprise? You could call it that. But Jake, she's gone; she's out of my life. I can be normal again. And thank you! Without you, I wouldn't be here at all. I'll never forget it . . . What? . . . Actually, if you can pick me up, I thought we might go to the police station and get that out of the way. Mom reminded me that we have to sign a statement. Would you have time to do that? Dad's going to check with them and see if today is okay . . . .Great! I'll call you as soon as I hear. Then there are the presentations tomorrow at work. If you like, we can go over those together. . . . .Yeah? Okay. I'll call you in a while."

As I turned away from the phone, Mom and Dad were standing there, smiling.

"What?" I said

"It sounds like you two get along well, now."

"We're just taking care of business, Mom"

"I see that," she said, and went about clearing the table.

Sunday turned out to be a full day. It felt good to be able to function in a productive way again without worry at every step. I got back to Jake, and we gave our statements at the police station. I brought the phone with me and whatever documents I had for them. They said they would let us know if they needed us for anything further, including a possible trial.

"When do you think I can have my car back?" I asked.

"In a couple of days." the policeman said. "We need to check it further for fingerprints and other things, in case she did have a helper. Thank you for coming in. And just so you know there was really no danger. It may have looked like a bomb but it was really just a rusty old pipe stuffed with soil."

As we left, Jake took my hand and said, "Library?"

I didn't need to be coaxed. I was anxious to add to the information I already had. Our decompression project was launched. We spent two hours there. Jake explored the book shelves, while I dove back into the archives and material on crashes, articles by pilots, experiences of passengers and reports by the NTSB, FAA and FBI. We figured if we split the labor it would save us some time.

Once we began, it was addictive. We were held captive by what we found. Although I was aware, for example, that the NTSB had full reign during its investigations, I learned they have more legal power than many government agencies. They can actually obtain subpoenas and court orders to question witnesses, inspect files and enter any facilities and aircraft, examine the computer data of any party involved in an airplane crash, and obtain any other relative information. With all that, when they investigate decompression or any other transportation accident, their final report establishes probable cause, from which they make recommendations for public safety. But it is not admissible in court, I read, nor is it their function to assign fault or determine civil or criminal liability. That would fall to the FBI, who would then pursue their own investigation.

There it is again -- everything has its function. I know where I've heard that before. I just didn't think it applied to groups and organizations.

After the library, we found we needed an energy boost, and stopped in a short-order place for hamburgers. As soon as we were seated, it was déjà-vu, and we both burst out laughing.

"We'd better pay attention when they bring the food this time," Jake said.

"By the way, I brought my notes with me for tomorrow's presentation. Would you like to go over them now?"

"Sure. Good thinking."

"Just keep the catsup off the pages, please."

"I can't promise, but I'll try," Jake said.

We spent the next two hours with questions and answers back and forth about our performance and presentation for work the next day. And after Jake drove me home, we parted promising to type up our notes for each other from the library research we did.

I said goodnight to Jake on the driveway, and he said, "Goodnight, Michelle Jamison. I had a good time. See you tomorrow."

40

We met at the college on this project for the last time. I hated to bother Dad, but I wouldn't be able to pick up the car for another day or so. When I got to the workshop, I found that most of the group had heard what happened with Sally. I was told it was on the evening news and in the morning paper.

"Wow," said Bob. "It says here her family has not seen her in over 10 years."

Before we even began the day, I was surrounded by my concerned co-workers.

"Michelle, we're glad you're here and that whole mess is over."

"Wow! What a thing to go through. What an interesting first week at work. Glad you're okay."

Everyone was talking at once. I'm not quite sure who said what first.

"Do you think she'll stand trial?" asked Chip.

"I doubt if she'll be found sane, but you never know," I said.

"Boy, Michelle, you had some Chicago welcome." said John. "What do you think of the city now?"

"It's my home. And I would miss not being here with all of you."

We gabbed a few minutes more, and then got down to business.

Once the implementation plan was completed, we summarized the spreadsheets and design proposals and made

the final presentation to management. We could hardly wait
for their decision. Now, we thought, there was nothing to do
but hold our breath until Tuesday morning.

It would have been worth waiting for, but as it
turned out, we didn't have to wait until Tuesday. When
management saw our proposal, the 70% material cost
reduction and the multi million dollar cost savings and our
implementation plan, they were speechless -- Dean most of
all. By afternoon, the place was buzzing.

While we were still together, Dean came in to thank
us, and I'm sure I detected tears in his eyes. He proceeded to
give us a little speech about how grateful he was for what we
had achieved, and in so short a time.

The workshop was over. It was time to integrate this
new design into our system. We didn't anticipate a great deal
of difficulty, but it was the next step, and it was all to begin
on Tuesday: setting up purchasing and costs; assembly line;
production time; packaging, delivery times and more. All the
departments were excited, and the whole company would be
a part of the team.

At the end of the day, John asked for our attention.
"I'm proud of you, as you know. I've never worked with any
team better than yours. You've made these sessions fun and
exciting as I watched your sharp minds at work. And I thank
you for your patience. I know it wasn't easy."

"Thank you again, everyone. Congratulations."

We again congratulated each other on our success. I
told John and the team, "I appreciated your concern so
much. It meant a lot to me." When I mentioned that it was
great working with them on this project, they responded
warmly.

Being hired by Alarum Aerospace was amazing;
being accepted by my co-workers was beyond wonderful,
because Jake isn't the only one who found a second home.

41

I was finally able to leave this building without having to look over my shoulder. I felt liberated. Jake caught up with me outside the door, where I had told Dad he could pick me up.

"Hey, hurry and catch your Dad right now, before he leaves. I can drive you home.

"That's okay, Jake, Dad doesn't mind."

"Honestly, it's not a problem."

"Well, thank you." I caught my dad just as he was ready to walk out the door. We started toward Jake's car.

"Isn't it great? The Michelle-shifts are canceled, and I'll be able to go to my car like a normal person again."

"That's too bad. I looked forward to it. Does that mean I'm out of an escort job, too?"

"Not unless you want to be bored to tears. But once in a while wouldn't hurt."

"I guess I'll just have to be satisfied with that."

"Do I still have your offer to help me with the decompression problem?"

"Of course. We can begin with finding out how our new inlet check valve works in that situation when it's ready. I think this project of yours will be interesting. Maybe we can even bring it in to Bob later, when things calm down at work, and get a team going on it. What do you think?"

"You read my mind. My plan was to gather as much material as I could, and do as much research as possible to build a strong case so that he might want to take it on. Of course, that depends on what we find."

"In the meantime, will we research again tomorrow night, or would you consider a movie?"

"I think we can take a break – as long as it isn't a horror movie."

"We'll manage to find something. How about if I pick you up around 7:00, and we'll grab a bite beforehand."

"Great! Sounds like a plan. Thanks, Jake."

"Gee, it looks like it's clouding up all of a sudden. Did they predict rain?"

"I don't think so, but that's not a guarantee." I smiled, and I couldn't stop smiling all the way home.

"It's nice to see you look happy after all you've been through, "Jake said.

"I feel as if I've started a new life. You know, I've always wanted to use that phrase. This time it really fits."

Half way home, the clouds moved in pretty fast, and the wind whipped up. There was the first splash on the windshield.

"This must be one of those pop-up storms," Jake said. "I hoped I'd get you home before any real downpour . . .or not. Oh-oh!"

By the time we reached the driveway, it was a monsoon. It was raining sideways.

"Thanks, Jake. I'll talk to you later."

"Wait!" he yelled.

Too late. I was already out of the car and ran into the house. In those two seconds, I was soaked. Mom came to the door.

"Oh, my God! Look at you! You look like a drowned puppy. Take those things off in the bathroom. I'll get your robe."

"Hi, Michelle. A little wet out there, is it?"

"Hi, Dad. Just a little."

The good food aromas flowed out of the kitchen and filled every room. You could tell Mom was at it again. Dinner was scrumptious, as usual. "Simple," as Mom puts it.

The menu tonight was Caesar salad, broiled sirloin steak, double baked potatoes and onion broccoli.

"I think you're setting me up, Mom, so that I'll never leave home."

"Well, no, but that's not a bad idea."

"By the way, I won't be home for dinner tomorrow night."

"What's up? " asked Mom.

"Something to eat and a movie with Jake." That was me trying to sound casual.

"Hmmm, I thought so. Not bad for a guy who almost got you fired."

"Mom, that's over."

"I know. Just teasing. He's very nice."

"Yes, he is, isn't he?"

"We cleared the table, I helped put the kitchen back in order, and I excused myself. "This is a good night to dig into the decompression stuff. I haven't had a chance until now to put some of my research together."

"Maybe I'm new and naïve in the industry, Mom, but I promised myself I would at least try my own investigation into the kind of situation that could have been fatal to me and everyone on my flight. It's not to prove myself at work, either. I couldn't help but feel way down in my gut that there's got to be something mechanical that can jump into action like a superhero when rapid decompression rears its ugly head. I've got to try for it even though the whole industry has tried to work their magic. The world laughed at a lot of people who had goofy ideas like mine, and they wound up hitting their targets. Maybe that's why fate brought me here, Mom. Who knows?"

42

While the storm raged outside, I settled down with whatever books and papers Jake and I had found so far. Reading about these tragic events that took place in the sky was heartbreaking. But as an engineer, I needed to remain objective. I also knew that the information I had here would not be enough, but it might lead me to other resources. That reminded me to call the airline to find out if the NTSB had issued their findings yet.

Going over some of this material, I started to think about the general lack of public knowledge of rapid decompression. Would it help save lives, I wondered, if passengers knew more about it and how to protect themselves before it occurred?

"Dad," I called. "Come here a second."

"What's the matter?"

"I just wanted you to listen to this. I never came across these facts about rapid airplane decompression before. This report says there are about 40 to 50 of these types of accidents a year. I guess that's not a lot compared to the number of flights. But if you're on a plane that's having one . . . Did you ever see any public information about one like the one I experienced coming home?"

"I don't think so."

"It goes on to say that if a plane is at a cruising altitude of 35,000 feet to 39,000 feet when decompression occurs, a healthy adult will die within a couple of minutes without oxygen. So you'd better get your oxygen mask on as fast as possible. And what's even worse is that only lasts for a few minutes while the pilot tries to drop the aircraft down to a breathable level, maybe 8000 feet. I'm sure most people don't know that. Maybe part of my mission should be to do some sort of ad campaign to get the word out."

"You'd better talk to your boss about that, Michelle. There might be protocol involved."

"This report also said you should keep your belt on throughout the flight, regardless of what the seat belt signs say. But you're right. Jake said to bring this to Bob, too. I don't want to step on any toes."

"You can do your homework, anyway. It couldn't hurt."

"Oh, I will."

"Something else, Princess?"

"I made some notes about my thoughts concerning the decompression issue and put them in some intelligent order that I could show to Jake tomorrow. The vision of what occurred on my plane won't leave me alone."

"You know, Michelle, you might still be stressed from that experience. Not only that, you had a double whammy when Sally came into your life. I would say that would all eventually fade, but I'm no professional. Why don't we give our doctor a call? You should go and have a talk with him. He might even refer you to someone. It could be that this decompression project of yours is the answer to relieving that stress. It'll keep you active and involved. But, Princess, let's make sure."

"Maybe, Dad. I'll see how it goes."

43

During the evening, I moseyed into the den where my parents were watching television. It was a sitcom that I guess they always caught this time of night on a Monday. But I couldn't focus. I waited until the ads came on before I bothered them with what I wanted to share.

"You know, I'm glad I went with this company. It's been an incredible experience so far, beyond what I ever expected."

"That is the best news, Michelle. I'm so happy it worked out for you," Mom said.

"What makes it unusual?" asked Dad.

"First of all, the people. In a short time, they became like a second family. They actually protected me from Sally. How often would that happen?"

"How often would someone like Sally happen?"

"True, but you know what I mean, Dad. And then there was Dean Davis, the Vice President. When he heard that we had achieved his goals, and then some, he came in person to speak to us. He was overcome with gratitude. Where do you find that kind of a man?"

"Now that is rare," Dad said.

"As I listened to him, I wondered if that man of vision understood what he did for my team, as well as the company."

"What do you mean?"

"Dad, the man initiated this workshop, chose us to learn this concept, and then insisted we move beyond what we ever thought we could do, in spite of our strong resistance in the beginning. I believe he sparked a cultural change in Alarum."

"I had many kudos, of course, for John, who was on the front lines, dealing with that resistance head on."

"Who's John, dear?" asked Mom

"He was our consultant, our leader, and the main reason, I think, for the team's success. Through his management and people skills, he gave us confidence. He opened up and expanded our individual creativity, and before we knew it, he guided us away from 'business as usual' to 'anything is possible.' He helped us break our old paradigms."

"We learned how to brainstorm and build on each other's ideas. I don't know how to explain it. It was like an extension of school, but in a much more dramatic and exciting way. We weren't just learning it; we were living it. We were able to cross-connect concepts and ideas to arrive at final designs and conclusions we could all agree on, and we took pride in our final accomplishment."

"But most of all, we learned to understand this whole system of Functions: Identifying verb-noun functions; building a FAST diagram, ranking functions for reality and category; and ranking functions for relative costs. All of that enabled us to come up with the result that floored management. It wasn't easy to learn, and it wasn't easy to convey, either. But John did it with clarity and patience."

I don't believe there are many companies today who give as much recognition to their employees and show such appreciation for loyalty and hard work as Alarum. Once and for all, I'm sure this is the place for me." I finished and drew a long breath.

Dad said, "Princess, I think we get that." They sat there and smiled at each other.

"What? You're doing it again. Why are you smiling?

Mom said, "You haven't talked non-stop like that since you were ten years old, and we took you to Disneyworld."

"Oh, guys, I'm sorry."

I didn't realize it, but I guess I talked my poor parents' ears off right through the commercial.

"Don't be silly. We're thrilled. And the boys will be, too. Wait till they hear. They're coming in soon. They said they can't wait."

"Oh, boy. Now I'm in for it!" I held my head.

"In for what?"

"Them!"

Mom and Dad both burst out laughing.

When they recovered, Mom said, "Somehow, I think you'll survive."

44

I was so function conscious, now, that whenever I thought about the decompression event that I experienced or anything for that matter, I couldn't help but wonder about the emotional damage that was done to passengers and how they functioned afterwards. I seemed to have handled it okay -- I think. Maybe Dad was right, and the jury is still out on that. Some of my research did talk about post-traumatic stress, and how it could be evidenced right away, while for some, it didn't show up until much later.

Would those more affected than I still be able to function afterwards in relationships and in their daily lives? What if they were analyzed by means of a Technical FAST Diagram? Would their basic function change or just their secondary supporting functions? Would they still be an important working part of the human "system," or would the diagram not work, proving them to be dysfunctional? Sally was one example of the effects of trauma, although she was mentally ailing and therefore vulnerable before the incident. For someone with that type of condition, I'm sure it must be worse. I felt even more of an urgency to pursue what I was trying to do.

I was ready to go to bed for the night, but I decided to take another look at the material I'd collected so far. Most of it had to do with fatal crashes, many of which affected the inflow and outflow valves. That's what kept me at the library so long, to search for more.

Mom and Dad were still awake, and as I began go over my notes, I thought they would be interested in hearing some of these amazing facts. They looked up as I walked into the den, papers in hand.

"Hi. We thought you were on your way to sleep," Mom said.

"I was, but I wanted look again at the report for Bob, in case there was something I could change or add. But you should see these statistics, Mom. They're so surprising."

Dad put down the newspaper he was catching up on during the TV ads. "It sounds like you're really moving forward with your project."

"I am. Listen to this. Did you know that the average annual risk of being killed in a plane crash is one in 11,000,000?"

"That is amazing," said Dad. "Most people would believe death in a plane accident would be a lot more eminent."

"But wait. The annual average risk in a car crash is one in 5,000. And an analysis of plane crashes between 1983 and 2000 found there was a 95.7% survival rate. Furthermore, in the U.S. in 2010, compared to the fatalities in motor vehicles, boats and trains, airplanes had the lowest number of all."

"So you're saying it's safer to crash in a plane?" asked Mom. "I wish I didn't know that."

"I doubt you'll have to worry, Mom. You'll be fine."

"Just kidding, Princess."

"Okay. I guess it is time for bed. Night all."

We exchanged hugs and kisses, and I went back to my notes. I wouldn't pop the decompression-project question tomorrow. The plant would be too busy with implementing our newly designed valve, and I'm sure Bob would be grumpy and a wild man getting back to his desk and work piled several feet high, according to him, to even think about anything else. A few day's wait, or even a week would be the prudent thing to do -- or maybe more? Jake and I will have to play it by ear.

But that doesn't make me less excited about the idea. I'll have plenty to do at home to finesse the work necessary to try to make the project seem feasible.

45

The atmosphere at the office this particular Tuesday was vibrant. The plant had a rhythm and a pulse. The implementation process had begun, and everyone was at work to make it a success. Even the Marketing Department, I was told, was preparing a campaign to jump-start aftermarket sales. It was a day when the whole company had put our team on a pedestal, and we felt like celebrities.

Members of the team who didn't work at our facility stayed one more day to see things launched and on their way. Douglas McNabb was thankful beyond words that, with the lowered cost of the valve, he would not have to oversee a move of the part assembly to the Mexican plant. He was even more grateful that he escaped having to lay off his second shift. *Good for you, Red.*

Just before lunchtime, an email came through for me. I was almost fearful of opening it, until I remembered that Sally was no longer a problem. It said:

"TO THE VA TEAM, Lunch at 12:15 at 'our restaurant'. BE THERE! You, too, Bob!"

I didn't know who thought of it, but aside from affirming to each other that we worked hard and did well, it was a chance to say good-bye to a few of the group we may not see for a while. Good idea!

We all seemed to emerge from the office about the same time. I guess we were all eager to say good bye to the team.

"Hey," said Randy, "Most of us seem to be here. Why don't we take two cars? It'll save time."

"Perfect," said Leland, "but where are Jake and Bob?'

"They might be a lost cause. I think we'd better go," suggested Doug.

It was a short distance, and parking wasn't difficult on the street. We started for the door just as Marie came out to serve a table.

"Hi, y'all. I see you made it back. Nice to see you."

Hi, Marie. You, too. There are five us, but two more may join us."

"Outside? Two tables?"

"I think so. The late-comers might be insulted otherwise."

Everyone agreed.

"Gotcha."

We arranged ourselves in the chairs around the tables, eager to talk. Everyone spoke at once. I couldn't hear above the din, but somebody had the good sense to talk louder than the rest and remind us to figure out what "we wanted to order, for heaven's sake." By the time Marie returned, we were ready for her.

Waiting for the food to come was another gabfest. Conversation turned to the workshop and our reactions to it. Each one around the table had something to say about how it affected him, personally. Then someone mentioned the certification exam. When will we know if we passed?

Randy said, "You know, it felt good to inject something new into the day-to-day operation of my department. It made me take a good look at the way we do everything. It was like I woke up to the smell of fresh coffee every morning and wanted to get going."

"I know what you mean," said Doug. "I had the same thought. And for the first time in a long while, I had the feeling that I was doing something important to help us and our company. It was like a rebirth."

"Funny you guys should say that. It was an epiphany for me, too," said Chip. "I even saw my customers in a different light. I thought I was serving them well before, but I can see where there could be a little improvement."

Everybody looked at Leland. "Well maybe I won't be as reluctant to speak up anymore, as I've always been."

"Oh, Oh! I think we created a monster!" Randy said.

"Honestly. I know that's always been my way, but I had fun interacting with you guys -- being noisy about salesmanship, brainstorming and all. And I feel as if I can loosen up and improve my work, now, and not worry about little things that bothered me before. It felt great to help us and our company. I believe we are a family, and we can't miss."

The whole table applauded. "Atta boy, Leland."

"Okay, Princess, your turn." Doug grinned and ducked.

They all said, "oooo!"

"You'd better hide," I told him with a smile.

"So, tell us, Michelle. How was this whole thing for you? You can probably give us the most objective answer."

I paused to collect my thoughts as I looked around the table. At that moment Bob and Jake appeared.

"Hey," said Chip. "Look who managed to escape."

There was another round of applause. Bob bowed to one and all as he and Jake took their seats.

"Hurry up and get your orders in, you two. Michelle works for a slave driver, and she has to get back to work."

"I never said that! You're a troublemaker, Chip Walters."

"That's okay, Michelle. I never believe him anyway, he's in sales. What were you all talking about when we got here?"

Chip turned serious. "The workshop, Bob, and what it did for us beside teaching us Value Analysis. Michelle was about take her turn when you walked in."

"Good. I'm glad we didn't miss that. Go ahead, Michelle."

"You mean beside learning VA first hand? That was an incredible opportunity I didn't think I would be given so soon. It taught me logic and organization -- never to miss a step when working on a project if you want a perfect result. Always follow the job plan and use all the tools. It reinforced my skills for academic arguments and discussions and to keep an open mind. It enabled me to know the people I work with better than I might have otherwise, and -- I learned to never judge a book by its cover."

I looked at Jake; he had a little extra color in his face.

"Jake?" said Chip. "How about you? It seems this workshop did something for us all in a personal way, as well as for our company. Did it affect you that way, too?"

"I have to say, Chip, it took me by surprise. I didn't expect the side benefits of Value Analysis. It taught me that I didn't know as much as I thought I did, and that there would always be something to advance engineering -- something new to keep the profession alive and exciting. And it gave me the confidence in myself to be able to accept that with an open mind and go with it. Then there are you guys. I feel closer to everyone on the team, too. It taught me to be a team player. It gave me a chance to know all of you better, and I'm glad to be here. One thing more, it taught me how to handle relationships, and to have all the information at hand before I make decisions."

Marie had come with the two late orders in the meantime, and everyone finished up, including Bob and Jake.

Bob checked his watch. "We really should be getting back, you know. The plant is humming."

"Oh, no you don't," said Randy, "It's your turn. The last person in the group to give us complete understanding of why our work was so important. It'll give us closure, Bob."

"Okay. What it did for me was to tell me what a great bunch you are. When we're in a cinch, you're there for us. I know I have a tendency to work only in my silo. And on occasion I may be a little difficult to work with. But you're hard work this week, and you never gave up, I learned something for myself, too, that I can't keep my nose in my desk all the time -- that if I lift my head and look around me, my job may even become easier by virtue of my colleagues that surround me every day, and what they may bring to the table. I won't fight change anymore, either. I know I'll be left in the dust if I do, and I'll miss out on the thrill of what could be. You could say my new basic function is 'encourage change.' And about what we've all just done for our company, I'm speechless. Sorry I missed what was said before I got here. But from the little I heard, it's not only what the workshop did for Alarum Aerospace, but what it did for us, as well. We learned to think in functions and challenged our paradigms. The whole thing was just win-win."

Everyone applauded once more. Bob calmly took his seat. Marie brought the checks. To everyone's surprise Bob took them all. We said fond good-byes to those going back to their own home bases, and we quietly left.

ABOUT THE AUTHOR

James Guyette married Julieta Leyva in 2007. His three children are Jillian (16) , Jacob (3) and Jacqueline (1). He calls Chicago's Lakeview neighborhood home.

After nearly a decade-long career with a major aerospace company he jumped into an opportunity in management consulting. Over the last 14 years has had the privilege of serving clients around the globe.

Today he is the Managing Director of 4OpEx, Inc., an Operational Excellence firm dedicated to leading small teams to BIG results. His email address is JamesGuyette@4OpEx.com.